Oct, 1983

To Loren —

It's good for me to know someone like you, for your energy and personality light up my day.

Love ya,

Fred

The Up & Outer

The Up & Outer

Fred Foster

Tyndale House
Publishers, Inc.
Wheaton, Illinois

Unless otherwise noted, all
Scriptures quoted are from
The Living Bible © 1971,
Tyndale House Publishers.
Other quotations are from
the *New American Standard
Bible* (NASB), © 1960,
1962, 1963, 1968, 1971 by
The Lockman Foundation,
La Habra, California.

Library of Congress Catalog
Card Number 80-51699.
ISBN 0-8423-7798-0, cloth.
ISBN 0-8423-7799-9, paper.
First printing, September
1980.
Printed in the United States
of America.

Although this is the trial of but one man,

it grieved the entire family.

To my daughter, Ann, who lived with daily unpredictability;

to my son, Kenneth, who struggled to hold a modicum of respect

for a father destroying his world;

and to my wife, sweetheart, confidante and best friend, Arline,

who hung on when most would have let go,

who boldly sought help and believed in miracles,

I dedicate this book.

These are the ones through whom new life is celebrated,

and these are the ones without whom there would be no victory.

CONTENTS

FOREWORD

This is more than a preface to a book. It is an introduction to a person. I want you to know one of the most authentic people I've met in years. He's become one of my best friends. Though I've known him for only a few years, it seems like I've always been his friend. He's one of those delightful people who is so open, free, and affirming that you can enjoy being yourself with him. He happens to be the remarkable man who wrote this impelling, you-won't-be-able-to-put-it-down book. I want you to see Fred Foster through the eyes of my heart.

You are about to read his own amazing story. You will laugh and cry, ache and reflect as you are irresistibly drawn into his mind and heart. This is no zippy success story burdened down with religious jargon. Here is a book that has both guts and gusto. And it's all true.

Fred is an all-stops-out kind of man. He lives life to the hilt. Whether he's playing golf, planning a television shoot, putting together a deal for a client, hosting a party, or responding to some human need, he's clicking on all cylinders. You never want to say, "Will the real Fred Foster stand up." He has stood erect, and you know you are in touch with a very real person. His enthusiasm is contagious, his warmth is disarming, and his joy is undeniable.

At first you wonder if this is one of those uniquely gifted people whose intelligence, personality, and affable charisma is the result of a charmed, easy life. But then you discover that he is a man who is what he is because of what he's been through. In his eyes you can see the rainbow sparkling through the rain of previous suffering.

Life went bump for him on bottom below bottom, not on Skid Row, but in the plush offices of New York's frantic commercial television advertising world and the expense account luxury of elegant bars and restaurants. The sophisticated dereliction of being up and out. What happened to him, his marriage and family, his career, and most of all, his self-esteem, is the startling story of this book.

The fun-loving, dynamic, self-accepting man I know now is the personification of the traumatic transformation that happened to him. The Eternal Mansmith has had him on the anvil and has forged and hammered out a very special renaissance person who is living life as it was meant to be lived.

Though this book is autobiographical, the hero is not the author. God is. Here is an account of how he performs his greatest miracle—the recreation of a human being. The result is no plastic saint. Fred's faith is genuine and sustained by a virile and vibrant relationship with God. He's one of those rare Christians whose conversion has not made him "religious" in any stuffy or negative sense. His battle with alcoholism will touch raw nerves in those suffering this sickness. But the account of his release will pack a wallop for every reader who longs to be set free to live. Whatever our brand of compulsion or distortion of the gift of life, we will find ourselves on these pages and discover how God can take the raw material of our needs and failures and mold the person we were destined to be.

Fred is now an elder in our church here in Hollywood. He is a new breed of adventuresome, innovative leader who believes that this is the most exciting decade for the church since Pentecost. His own profound experience with God has made him a winsome witness who has helped countless people to find freedom and joy. As a leader he is helping to shape our church as a laboratory of new life where people can receive unqualified love, express their needs, and begin an abundant life.

What you are about to read has the undeniable marks of a gifted writer. The author's graphic, pictorial language puts the reader into every situation. This real-life account is like a fast moving river. The currents will catch you in the first pages and carry you on with "you are there" identification. When you finish you will feel that you have lived inside the skin of a broken person who was made whole. You will be left breathless as you run with the author as he ran from God, and then *to* God. There will be the deep satisfaction that comes from an intimate encounter with an honest person who has opened his mind and heart and shared the difficulties and delights of being human. You'll be left with a lingering question that will collect residuals for a long time to come: Can what happened to Fred Foster happen to me? That may even lead to a deeper question: Why not?

Lloyd John Ogilvie

PREFACE

This is not an exposé of the advertising business, nor is it a denunciation of television commercial film production. Both industries have been, and remain, the work in which I am proudly engaged.

I don't deny that advertising and film production offered the unusual opportunity and financial means through which my introduction to excessive living came. I do deny generalizing however, since my view of New York City is not New York City in the eyes of anyone else. An uncontrollable malady governed my sight and effectively dimmed my awareness of the normal people from whom I so desperately sought escape. Many drinkless months passed before I began to recognize the greater truths of our industry.

Advertising and television certainly do not need me as their defense spokesman, for to no less a degree excessive life-styles must exist in other business fields. We who look for escape from reality, who turn to like companions in support of our quest, and who listen only to what we shout about ourselves—and thus fail to see the person we really are—surely must be in neighborhoods throughout our land. Put me in any one of them and I would tell this same story.

I became an up and outer, once my eyes were opened to the higher standard, because of decisions I made. Nothing less. It was through free will I chose to live beyond normality, and it was that same free will, turned around, which set me on a course which allowed this book to be written.

At no time during its writing was it ever my intention to discredit people, places, or vocations; many sequences of events and names of some people involved have been altered.

Fred Foster

You will stagger
like a sailor tossed
at sea, clinging to
a swaying mast.
And afterwards
you will say,
"I didn't even
know it when they
beat me up. . . .
Let's go and have
another drink!

PROVERBS 23:34, 35
THE LIVING BIBLE

GOD THE VOID

I don't know how long they had been following me. Without warning, two men from the Seventh Avenue and Forty-second Street crowd had come along each side of me. I felt their bodies against mine as they kept pace with my faltering steps. Firmly and persuasively, they each took one of my elbows. Just my elbows.

"Come with us, man. You've got what we want."

I looked at each of them. Fear possessed me. Nobody on this people-jammed street was even vaguely aware of my crisis. I saw no help from the crowd. Nathan's Restaurant, with its grotesque oversized hot dog sign, the line-up of cheap movie houses with their blizzard of lights, the adult bookstores, screaming for attention—all pretended not to see me. On Forty-second Street, at this time of night, you mind your own business and stay out of all trouble if possible.

"We ain't foolin', man. We each gonna drop you right here unless. . . ." Not the way a successful television commercial film salesman like myself would choose to die, I thought.

A sharp point touching my right side jolted me ahead of them. I lunged into the street traffic just as a Yellow Cab blared by. The *Daily News* truck slowed as I ran in front of it. Its angry driver sped up as soon as I passed, telling me that I wasn't being followed. I paused at the yellow center line long enough to see that the oncoming lane of Forty-second Street traffic was clear and rushed to the other side before I turned to see where my two assailants were. The twilight jungle had engulfed them. I broke into an easy jog, still feeling their anger for eluding them.

The Port Authority bus terminal and my yellow bus to freedom were in sight, but my racing heart forced me to slow to a fast walk. Pushing rudely against oncoming people, I moved toward the curb to gain open space and a clearer path.

I glanced behind. They were not following. Fear turned to exhilaration as I realized the old Brooklyn "run into traffic" maneuver had worked, a ruse I had last used when I was eleven years old, when cornered by a hostile gang under the Third Avenue elevator.

Inside the bus terminal, I moved to the nearest wall and put my back to it. I looked into the faces of the crowd for the two large men, my assailants. Other commuters were not paying any attention to me.

The street victory was now sweet. I had, in my inflated opinion, just displayed unusual bravery, and reasoned that I deserved a reward. I headed for my favorite terminal bar. This was turning out to be a very exciting Friday night— and I wasn't even home yet.

The bedroom was familiar, but silent and unhappy. I felt a troubled stillness. The grey light of early morning painted the ceiling a dirty white. My eyes began to focus. The dressers and chairs stared at me from their corners. They appeared uneasy with the tension of the room. I felt it also, and turned to my wife's side of our queen-sized bed. It was empty. Cold. I was alone. I knew why.

Arline could not even sleep in the same bed with me now. The touching and caressing of earlier love was gone. Was it because of how I had come to her last night? How frightening to feel this deep loss.

Losing was not my game—yet in my compulsion to win, I had lost. But only for a moment, I thought. I had pulled myself out of bigger jams than this one. I'll find the way to make this day come together. I wondered when I was going to stop getting myself into such messes. I remembered last night's escape from Forty-second Street. But what had happened after that? I asked myself.

Pieces of memory came back. When I finally got home, we had gone to a dinner party at the Bennetts'. We had walked to their house. Too bad we didn't take the car—I would have driven home, since I was in no condition to walk. It was an old and bad joke, but I forced a chuckle. I had to be nice to myself and laugh at my jokes, because Arline certainly wasn't being nice. She had moved to the spare bedroom.

I rose, and aimed silently toward her retreat. As I opened the door, she rolled her back to me as though turning in sleep. I knew she was pretending. Avoiding contact. The hurt struck the pit of my already troubled stomach as I realized we were farther apart than we had ever been. I had my work cut out for me if this day was going to be saved. It was now my turn to retreat.

The "happy-face" kitchen clock smiled eleven minutes after seven. I thought of turning it upside-down just to see how sad that silly face would look. Better not! Nobody would appreciate my sense of humor this morning. I had done enough damage for one weekend.

As I placed the water on for tea, I was greeted by another happy face. This one was alive, loaded with energy, golden brown, and needing to be let out of the house. Golden Retrievers love everyone, so I wasn't flattered by his circling display of affection. I let him out, and while standing at the door, I checked the weather.

Air Force pilot training had introduced me to weather forecasting. I was intrigued with its mysteries from the first day of preflight classes. From our back porch, I saw the tall, seventy-five-year-old oak trees stretching to touch the blue cloudless sky of a crisp October morning. It's going to be a beautiful fall day in New Jersey, and I felt better, despite the silent storm raging between Arline and me.

I knew how badly I had treated my body last night, although not much of the rest was clear. I recalled some of the evening, then stopped. It was much too uncomfortable. I heard Arline move back into our bedroom.

I prepared her tea, with honey and milk as she likes it. Her stirring upstairs told me this was for her a work day in Manhattan. She had returned to the world of fashion, seeking her own identity and to get away from my self-destruction.

To me her preparations signaled a free day in which to do whatever I desired. No one could have at that moment convinced me that I faced a day more dangerous than any of the thirty-five bombing missions I piloted over Nazi Germany. The worst which could have happened then was a hero's death. To be forced to live with present mistakes and failures bestows no honor or glory. The tea shook in its cup.

In our bedroom I felt the tensions, and counted on the tea offering to improve the atmosphere.

"Here's your tea, sweetheart." My voice was strong.

A discontented "Thank you" was my reward for the room service. Not a very nice tip.

"Hey, what's the matter? Did I do something wrong last night?"

"If you don't know, then we really are in trouble."

"I'm sorry if I went overboard." My voice was not as strong.

Turning to me for the first time, she showed the hurt on her face and in her eyes. "It's not just that, Fred. It's all of it put together. The way we live, and what you're doing to yourself and to the four of us."

"Come on, honey," I tried. "There's nothing wrong with our life. If I spent too much time with Ruth last night, I'm sorry. There was nothing to it. I wasn't trying to hide anything. I simply talked with the girl—that's all. And we were right in the living room—in full view of you and everyone else. Besides, you know I love you."

I looked for some softening in her face. There was none. Was I losing my touch? I moved toward her.

"Please don't tell me you love me. I really can't stand it right now. And don't try to put your arms around me as though I'm some kind of child who needs *your* help."

I withdrew my arms. I felt terrible. Dirty. Guilty. Rejected. She turned away, and I retreated to the other bathroom.

The hot water and the confinement of the shower stall surrounded me. I felt better. Cleaner inside. The sweet-tasting water cleared my mouth and teeth of last night's booze and cigarettes. My face was waking up. It had better. I remembered Abe Lincoln's remark that, after forty, everyone is responsible for his own face. My eyes stung. Here comes sobriety. I can feel it. One more victory to add to last night's on Forty-second Street. Too bad I couldn't "run into the traffic" to escape the problem I was facing with Arline.

She had to be met, and somehow won. In my opinion, there was no one to whom I could turn for help. Certainly no one interested in my problems.

I needed somehow to fill the void within me—and I didn't even know where to begin.

*What you do
with your problem
is far more
important
than what
your problem
does to you.*
ROBERT H. SCHULLER[1]

MY KIND OF FISH

As we drove into Manhattan, I tried pleasant conversation.

"What a beautiful day. I think I'll get the kids to help me with raking leaves today, hon."

Silence.

"It's a terrific day for it. I'm going to get out the hibachi and charcoal. We'll do a little hot dog cooking in the back-yard."

Silence.

"As a matter of fact, sweetheart, the three of us will come and pick you up tonight. Maybe we could all stop for dinner on the way back. OK?" I was excited about this thought.

From the corner of my right eye, I caught the half shake of her head. She was putting up with me. Finally she said, "I'm sure they would love that." Firm silence.

I dropped her off at the corner of Fifty-sixth Street and Fifth Avenue with the promise that I would be there to get her at five forty-five this evening. I watched as she was swallowed by the store employee's entrance. Suddenly I was alone.

A feeling of great freedom engulfed me. I couldn't contain the excitement building within me. There were no thoughts of Ann or Ken or leaf raking or hot dogs or dinners together. My mind was immediately saturated with being on my own. "I don't have to answer to anyone for the entire day," I shouted. I didn't think anyone heard me, but I know now that someone within me did—a partner, but not a friend—yet someone with me in my quest for freedom. Unaware of what was really going on inside me, I simply wanted to get out of Manhattan as fast as I could.

Crosstown traffic was still very light as I turned the Ford station wagon west and aimed for the Lincoln Tunnel. It felt good being on the streets of New York in my own car, secure in the knowledge that I could go anywhere I wanted.

There was cash in my pocket, credit cards with some power remaining, and self-confidence in my ability to alter this morning's rejection. I passed familiar corners, remembering some of those late nights I frantically searched for cabs, trying to get the last bus back to New Jersey. I remembered a few times taking the cab all the way home, and the money deals I made with the all-night drivers. But now I'm driving. I'm in control. My ego is being fed its breakfast in preparation for the rigors of the day ahead of me.

Emerging from the Lincoln Tunnel, I opened my window to smell the New Jersey air, which to me is cleaner, fresher, and more reviving than on the other side of the Hudson. I didn't care what others thought of our air. Out of the city now, I plunged into the meadows through which the turnpike sped. Industry was occupying more and more of the wild marsh lands. On the land not yet claimed, long brown spikes of cattails swayed and rippled in the October air gusts; reminding me of an ocean swell and Nantucket Island. I replaced that painful thought with the exhilarating prospects of where I was heading today.

The turnpike exit which would lead me home appeared. I speculated about our two children, Ken and Ann. Would they still be at home when I arrived? Distrust of their concern for me and second thoughts about their wanting to spend the day raking leaves were reasons I now used to justify a detour. I veered back onto the turnpike and continued west to another familiar exit. Three miles later, I spotted my first stop.

My favorite fishmonger welcomed me into his spotlessly clean market. I kicked the floor sawdust with authority and opened the nearest bin of fish. I wanted bluefish today because they're in season. I was again reminded of the beach home we still owned and the bluefish Ken and I had caught off the Nantucket shores.

I knew if we ever lost our Nantucket vacation home it would remain a cancer in our marriage. As I chose the fish I would have for lunch, I was able to push that negative thought from my mind. If Ann and Ken were not going to be home, I certainly wasn't going to charcoal hot dogs for myself.

"What commercials can I look for now, Mr. Foster?" The fishmonger weighed my choice as we talked about my film successes.

"The new Pepsi ones on the air now. They're mine."

"Do you want me to fillet this for you?"

"No. We had a crew in Florida last week on Schlitz. You'll see them in about six weeks."

He knew me to be a very prosperous film producer. I had conditioned him to that image of myself. It had taken a sizeable collection of fish to create the image—but I like fish and I found it easy to tell stories. My rationale was that he enjoyed knowing someone in "show biz." He felt I was his contact to firsthand information about the entire film industry. I sometimes included Hollywood star stories that I heard were being shot by other film companies. My stories were always true in fact. It was just that they were usually not personal experiences. These Hollywood shoots took more time to tell, so they only surfaced when he did the filleting for me. In truth, I needed this fish more than he needed my stories, for without the fish, I had no reason for the next purchase I planned to make.

I stepped outside and quickly pushed aside the stabbing thought of again having been a phony—a very disturbing realization. I refused to listen to it. Yesterday I was a phony. Today is real, and I'm on my own for the day. I have earned this day through work and worry and long hours in the wilderness of Manhattan. I deserve a rest from failure and bill collectors. My already high blood pressure rose as I pondered the change in direction the day was taking. Without hesitation, I turned the corner and quickly strode toward the satisfaction of my primary craving. It was impossible for me to know I was keeping a date with the driving voice within me. Despite what I said, I was not really in control. Something else inside me was.

The feeling came over me of being a bachelor again, a sensation of being in some distant land, of not being known by anyone. I was in the Air Force again, living in bachelor officer's quarters. Back then, I answered to no one about my personal life. Now for the next six hours, I would live back there in the past where I had no responsibilities. Where it was comfortable. I'd get away from people who know me intimately. From my family. I had stopped being able to deceive them a long time ago. They know me for what I really am, for they have seen the real me at home. I pushed that exasperating thought out of my mind, too. I didn't need such candor right now—I needed wine to go with the fish.

Going into liquor stores is supremely enjoyable. There's a musty, moldy, strong-smelling aroma within which reminds me of cocktail lounges and carefree hours. This one was no exception.

"The Mountain Chablis today, Mr. Foster?"

The owner had recognized me. He knew my name, and he knew my wine. I wonder if he was aware of a deflated ego which needed fresh hot air? If my ailment showed, he was treating it professionally.

He opened the extraordinarily large refrigerator door and emancipated a half-gallon bottle of chablis. The grapes had been grown, processed into wine, and bottled just for my lunch and this moment of truth.

"These California wines are coming into their own now," he said. "You'll enjoy it, I'm sure."

This unique wine merchant not only treated the wine with respect. He made me feel I had good taste, obviously born of familiarity with that life-style.

"We're expecting guests this afternoon," I said easily. "This should be enough if they take it easy."

"If not, just give us a call and we'll be glad to deliver anything at all. Ice, beer. . .you just call me, Mr. Foster. And charge it if it's more convenient."

We understood each other. He's the merchant—I'm the customer. The king. The boss. The one to be pleased. This man knows what he's doing. His efforts will be rewarded with future business. I left the store feeling important.

With food and drink clutched in my arms, I knew security. My mind raced towards lunch in anticipation of tastes and smells so much a part of "the good life." Today is enjoyable already. It's made for me. To be free. Yes, that's it—freedom. No one keeping score of my actions. I could not know that the cork in the bottle and the key to my prison were the same. I headed for the car.

The back door of our three-story colonial home was unlocked. Ann and Ken must be out. The empty kitchen and used breakfast cereal dishes confirmed it. The high school football game had priority. Our team played at home today, so they were involved in pregame fun. Good. Now I can become involved in my own priorities. My goal is in sight with no one else on the field. Not for the moment at least.

Broiled bluefish, done in melted butter and dillweed, will be it today. A simple lunch, and yet very low in carbohydrates. I wanted to lose weight and help lower my blood pressure, so I kept trying to maintain the "Drinking Man's Diet" I discovered months before.

I had probably heard about it at some bar where it may have made that night's drinking easier. It prescribed high protein and very little bread, sweets, or starch in any form. It was labeled the "Drinking Man's Diet" because one could drink as much liquor as desired because alcohol does not contain any carbohydrates. The entire study was one born of genius, I reasoned. The thought of losing weight by simply not eating the olive at the end of the martini appealed to me. It was a sacrifice a weaker man could not manage. I laughed heartily while the bluefish went under the broiler.

I had immediately refrigerated the wine upon arriving, so it was at the correct temperature as I retrieved it from its cold berth. I checked my wristwatch. Eleven o'clock already. Not too early for a small drink. Eleven need not really be considered morning drinking. Not on Saturday. Hundreds of thousands were drinking this very hour, at football games all over the East coast. I will drink a toast to victory with them and kill the thought of morning drinking.

I know that men who drink early may have a problem with drinking and need that first drink to get them going. I see them in the seedy bars of Manhattan on my way to work. Each time I catch sight of them I thank God that I don't have their problem. I didn't crave this wine today. The fish demanded a white wine, and while the broiling was proceeding, this first glass would only help pass the time. As it hit my stomach it ignited a fire straight from hell. And I calmed down. My unseen, unheard partner was pleased.

One quart of the half-gallon bottle was gone before I started to eat. I had long ago reasoned—and today believed—that drinking a half gallon of wine did not belong in the category of heavy or serious drinking. I switched to wine so as not to get drunk. This was not drinking. It was eating and also drinking. It proved later to be the fuse that started a deadly chemical reaction throughout my entire body. It flipped on the compulsive switch I didn't yet know was there. In trying to control my drinking through the type of drink I chose, I had already lost all control.

It was one-thirty. The happy-face clock looked much happier than it did this morning, and I had no desire to turn it upside-down. It was now a friend smiling approval. The banquet of bluefish gone, I turned to the wine. It was gone. So quickly. I raised the empty bottle over my head to allow the last few drops to trickle over my reaching tongue. Against the sunlight I saw that it was completely dry. I felt absolutely fantastic and believed all would soon be well between Arline and me.

The euphoria which I had come to love so much arrived, signaling a feeling of deep satisfaction in my life. I was no longer bored. Fear left, and took with it apprehension, panic, and insecurity. I was supreme master in my own disorganized prison without knowing my hands and feet were tied. I was a very happy man as I looked about at all I possessed in this lovely home.

A haunting fear of the Internal Revenue Service taking the house for unpaid taxes surfaced. I thought momentarily of our many other threatening creditors. I'll pay them all in the order of how loud they scream. But not on Saturdays. Creditors do not scream on Saturdays. Since church is not a creditor, even though we're behind in our pledge, Sunday is free of their persistence too. The outdoors beckoned.

My ego needed another charge, and the expanse of our property, so large to me and my Brooklyn past, always helped. The huge, indestructible old oak trees give me a feeling of stability as I pass them. At the end of our property, I turned and faced the house, two hundred feet away. Breathless with pride, I viewed the magnitude of my ascension in life. I did not see the badly chipped paint, peeling from windows and sills. Ugly red rust stains on the dirty white stucco sides did not capture my attention. I ignored the eroding gutters and split downspouts. I saw the house completely and beautifully restored. I also discovered the martini cocktail in my hand.

I had mixed a vodka martini before venturing into the cold October air. Pleased with my unconscious thoughtfulness, I finished the drink and raised the empty stem glass in salute to the land and trees and house over which I have domain. Fear of losing it all gripped me. My mind searched for a strategy to success and a brilliant plan was born.

*Life is what
happens to you
while you are
making plans.*
ANONYMOUS

THE GRAPE PRODUCES JELLY

I found it difficult to be calm as answers came to me in rapid succession. For fifteen years, Arline had wanted me to save money each week. She hadn't asked for large savings—just often. "A few dollars each payday. That's all. You'll be surprised how quickly it will add up. And I'll feel so much better knowing we have something to fall back on," she pleaded.

I never answered her plea. My stratagem for financial security has always been based upon someday earning more money than we could spend. It seemed to me that savings would then automatically accrue from the surplus cash we had each week. Even I knew this wasn't logical, but it had helped to put one fear of the future away. Now my drugged mind was telling me to listen to my wife.

Monday morning I will open a savings account. I'll open it in Manhattan, close to the studio office so I can make weekly deposits easily. Fifty dollars each week should do it. Perhaps that's not enough. I'll make it seventy-five. Not too

shabby, I thought. I marveled at how much would accumu-
late in five years. The thought of ten years staggered me.
Plan number one was on its way. Time for a short drink.

No more of those martinis, though. At least not at home
because I had promised Arline I would stop drinking them.
I knew she thought I had agreed to stop drinking gin completely. My crafty use of the promise consisted of not drinking martinis when at home. The oath didn't hold for New
York City. During the five-day workweek, the clients upon
whom I call need martinis to get through lunch. We look
upon the drink with much respect, and refer to it often as
"white lightning" or "loud-mouth soup," for those not
capable of control when imbibing. To vow not to drink a
martini during lunch would assure me of expulsion from
fellowship with men I consider true and noble friends. I
could scarcely be expected to enforce such a pledge. And I
didn't. I switched drinks—at home. To Canadian Club
manhattan cocktails. They're only ninety proof—the same
as any bottle of vanilla extract.

Canadian Club whiskey may not do the same job in a
cake or a pudding, but it brings on a nicer tasting world for
me. This one was going down particularly easy, and I didn't
think it was lethal. Gin is lethal. I further reasoned that I
had honored my promise to Arline by staying away from the
gin, ignoring the refueled flames in my stomach ignited
earlier by the wine and vodka. My heart raced with the
new alcohol as plan number two flashed across my mind.

To ensure the success and practicality of the new savings
plan, on Monday morning I am going to hit the streets of
Manhattan as they have never before been hit. I'm still one
of the best commercial film salesmen in the business, and
every advertising agency on Madison Avenue is going to
know exactly how proficient I am. Every possible lead to
new business I will follow. My relentlessness will become
legend. Management will be concerned about the added
commission provision in my contract. It's going to cost
them fifteen thousand dollars more than they had planned.

That size bonus will certainly provide for the family. I may even have to find an additional avenue of capital investment. The stock market? No. That will have to wait until the house is redecorated and the kitchen enlarged. This is the second time today the house has been painted. Our problems are improving now in triplicate.

Three of a kind is worth betting in any poker game, and the third courageous card shown to Arline tonight will be controlled drinking. I didn't know the sole incentive for controlled drinking grew from the reality that I lose control over my drinking the moment of taking the first drink. I simply wanted to impress Arline with the seriousness of my first two new directions to success and security. Recently she has stopped commenting on my drinking, but most of our marriage has been peppered with annoying remarks before, during, and after drinking bouts. Controlled drinking will put an end to all doubts she may still have concerning my habit. Control would be easy. Change is the order of the day.

At the risk of offending a few drinking clients, martinis will have to go at lunch. I'll continue to drink with them after work, so business will not be affected too much. I'll compromise for lunch. Wine only from 12:30 to 2:30 should not offend. I'll still be drinking along with them even though wine is not considered alcohol in these circles. The afternoons will be available for sales calls as a result of the shortened lunches. Two more hours of screenings and sales opened up for me. My work day had almost doubled. So should my income. And my prestige.

In quick succession, I proved I could do anything to which I had set my mind. Unquestionably no help was needed from anyone. I continue to be the self-made man, the Flying Fortress pilot of old.

My plans for the future were suddenly halted as seventeen-year-old Ann came in. After a quick hello and knowing glance at the full cocktail glass, the empty wine bottle, and the dirty kitchen, she vanished into the upper rooms of the house. She made me aware of the time. It was nearing four o'clock—time to leave for New York. While putting the kitchen back in order, I pondered why Ann had not told me who won the game. Surely she knew I was interested. I worked hard enough to justify that claim, and she had no complaints with regard to her living conditions. Children in this town have had too much given to them. I was annoyed that Ann was like the rest of them.

I knew if I arrived late in New York, Arline would think I had been drinking. Today's consumption totaled one martini—outside the house—and two manhattans—inside the house. Wine with the bluefish was its partner in nutrition, not an alcoholic beverage, so I felt good about being quite sober. I wanted, and needed, a clear head when presenting the exciting discoveries of the afternoon, thus it pleased me that—in my opinion—I had not drunk too much. I enjoy the friendship of those fifteen drinking buddies who all drink more than I. Compared to them, I'm doing fine and could see no problem.

Little did I know then how comparing myself to others was damaging me. Dietrich Bonhoeffer said, "If my sinfulness appears to me to be, in any way, less detestable in comparison with the sins of others, I am still not recognizing my sinfulness at all."[2] I compared my actions to those I looked upon as worse, or lower, than mine, never to the higher standard I should be meeting. Many of my city colleagues remained overnight in hotels when we were out too late. Some of them didn't get home for days. A few couldn't make it to work the next day. Not me! Perhaps I did my wife and family an injustice by not staying out all night, I realized, after learning the next day the condition in which I arrived home some nights.

There weren't too many New Jersey bus commuters dropped off at their front doors late at night by a New York/New Jersey bus. On a few occasions, when I had passed out (I used to say fallen asleep) and been aroused ten miles beyond my exit point, the sympathetic driver would take me back home en route to his garage. His only other choice was to let me out in the middle of some small New Jersey farm town where everyone was by then slumbering. On cold winter nights, it would take an even colder heart to leave me with no way back. When I would leave the bus voluntarily under these circumstances, it was because I would not admit my error to the driver. My pride demanded normal behavior, so I would call Arline in the middle of the night to come after me, or when fortunate, find a taxi and gladly spend the twenty or thirty dollars to get home unaided. This I believed to be normal behavior.

The fact that I left home precisely at four o'clock for this journey into New York City did not seem strange, either. I know normal people would not allow two hours to travel sixteen miles unless they planned to walk. I wasn't walking, but I did think it wise to consider the possibility of a flat tire or a traffic jam en route. That I have never had a flat tire on this present two-year-old car, or that the probability of a traffic jam on Saturday afternoon was very slim, did not rule out the likelihood either condition could happen. I refused to consider the odds, and chose to be prepared for any one of these common hazards. A far greater hazard awaited. I thought I was prepared.

The massive four-lane ramp which raises thousands of cars, trucks, and buses over the streets and business district of Union City, New Jersey, is the principal entryway to the Lincoln Tunnel. Rain, sleet, snow, ice, and salt pounded by countless tires had created potholes which were the "daddies" of all potholes. Dodging these monsters to and from work each day has become routine for most commuters. I too can maneuver around them with great skill, and enjoyed some of the close encounters. I didn't enjoy hitting the rather large hole which exploded beneath me and shook the station wagon into the adjoining lane. It wasn't serious. The car ran smoothly again, and all was well. But now I had a reason to stop. The tire must be inspected before I risk putting Arline in this vehicle. I knew precisely where to pull up, and without preparation, encountered the ultimate hazard to driving in our land. A drunk.

The cocktail lounge of this urban hotel does not attract many during Saturday afternoons. This is one of the reasons I like coming into it. Other reasons have been because the bartender knows how to mix martinis properly, he knows me, the music is kept low in volume, it's a quiet place, it's close to New York City, it's easy to park. Any reason is a good reason. I had used them all on previous Saturdays. But today I had a new rationale. The car may have been damaged. That it really wasn't didn't diminish the logic of the incident validating my afternoon detour.

With a nod, I requested a double vodka on the rocks. The bartender placed a drink before me. He knew what I wanted. I only had to let him know the pattern had not changed. It pleased me to be known in yet another cocktail lounge. I tried to relax. Still plenty of time.

It takes only a few minutes to drive through the tunnel and into Manhattan. Arline will not finish her work for at least ninety more minutes. I can use this time to review my exciting plans before they're presented. I signaled for another drink. It appeared smaller, and half of it vanished with my first sip. Were my sips getting bigger? My need greater? I searched my mind for those new programs of success I had put together earlier. Thoughts evaded continuity. Would not come together clearly. I felt guilty. Defeated again. This pattern had become more noticeable to me lately, and I could not cope with the depression which comes so often after spectacular and brilliant thoughts of achievement. I was very uncomfortable. Guilt came in a stem glass. So will courage if I order one more. I nodded. Self-confidence returned as quickly as the third vodka disappeared and I started for the parking lot.

I didn't want to be late. To be late would endanger the scene of calmness and sobriety I planned when I met Arline. I headed for the tunnel and Manhattan.

Driving is an excellent test of sobriety. I pride myself on

being a superb driver under all conditions—with or without drinking. Today was no exception. All oncoming objects were in focus. My head began to clear as I gulped the fresh air swirling throughout the station wagon. I had opened all windows and now felt the coldness of the October air. Cold air smells cleaner to me and seems to force more oxygen into my lungs. I had smoked too many cigarettes during that last stop and needed to be cleaned out inside. I charged into the Lincoln Tunnel. The noise was deafening. Fifty miles an hour through the confines of the Lincoln Tunnel with all windows open is not the way to find serenity. The cold air didn't smell very fresh in here. First a truck, then a Jersey-bound bus flashed by in the opposite lane. The swirl of air behind them sucked dust and debris from the car floorboard. Dirt flew into my face and eyes. I swerved into the opposite lane—but only partially and only momentarily. Shaken by this near-tragedy and the pothole jolt still fresh in my memory, I slowed down considerably. I was awake. Sober.

It was not yet five o'clock when I parked on Fifty-sixth Street. Crosstown traffic had been light. So was my head after that close call in the tunnel. Another victory. I closed and locked the car and headed for another of my favorite routine stops. The victory demanded a reward.

"At a certain point in the drinking of every alcoholic, he passes into a state where the most powerful desire to stop drinking is of absolutely no avail. This tragic situation has already arrived in practically every case before it is suspected."[3] The book *Alcoholics Anonymous* made this statement many years before I knew why it was not possible for me to stop today. The compulsive drinking switch had been turned on by the first glass of wine before lunch. The "Drinking Man's Diet" would now continue, and considerably more would be lost than a few pounds of fat.

A new peace settled over me. I had made it on time and would be here when Arline appeared on the scene. What a great joy—and what a great time for a quick drink! I knew exactly where to go. After all, I spent many hours walking these sidewalks. This was my part of town, my working and drinking neighborhood. I knew the buildings. I knew the ones in which to hide for a few minutes or a few hours. They're friendly. They accept me, indifferent to my compulsive needs.

A half-block off Madison Avenue on Fifty-fourth Street, I saw its awning jutting to the street curb. I pictured every detail of its warm, intimate bar. I almost trotted as I plunged headlong towards my only way to facing life. Just before reaching the awning, I slowed to a walk and entered slowly. The impression of casually killing some time during a lazy Saturday afternoon was my intent. I knew these bartenders. They were my friends during the work week. They knew me to be a solid film executive without a problem to his name. No need to have them think I had been near a drink all day.

Even though I was now very near Arline, and could be there in less than two minutes, I had to plan carefully the remaining forty minutes of freedom. I would leave here precisely at 5:35 and buy a cup of black coffee at the drug store close to her building. Then, with coffee in hand, I would look to all of New York as though I had been hanging around for some time before meeting my lovely blonde wife.

I would stick to vodka, but now asked that an onion be included. The small pickled onion would help my breath. Coupled with the smell of coffee, that would help me pass for a recent visitor to McDonald's.

I kept to my plan. At exactly 5:35 I left the bar, but not until I had systematically consumed three very large doses of vodka and onions. The last one was not part of my original plans.

The euphoria returned. Elation filled every part of my body and mind. Arline no longer worried me. She would be thrilled about the future I had discovered for us today. That I was unsteady in my walk to get the coffee did not dim the pride I felt because I would not drink much after today. I remembered that new resolve and was determined to keep it. The coffee would do the job on my unsteadiness and the coffee beans would assure the loss of all telltale breath odors. I put two beans in my mouth and chewed the bitter seed before drinking its brew.

I tried desperately to keep from swaying and to focus on the activity around me. I cursed myself for drinking that last double and took the coffee more intently. The beans in my mouth interfered. I spit them into the gutter and swallowed the remains of the hot liquid. Where is sobriety?

The hour of Arline's appearance arrived. I was not ready for it. The coffee had not brought sobriety. Euphoria vanished. Bertrand Russell said that "life is a bottle of very nasty wine." My life had become nasty through a bottle of very good wine, and now I had to face Arline.

My alcohol-soaked mind could only focus on putting up a good front to dupe Arline into believing my day had been filled with the Saturday chores as a faithful husband. I finished the remaining coffee and leaned against the car. This was too uncomfortable. I had to move—to test my ability to walk without weaving. It wasn't too bad. I convinced myself that all was well. The subterfuge would succeed. Excitement regarding our future faded. I felt insecure about my presentation to her.

Someone once said that the ultimate rejection comes when your psychiatrist commits suicide. Whoever said that had not dreamed dreams from the high alcohol-induced plateaus as I had done today. To me, the ultimate rejection comes when an alcoholic faces himself honestly for the first time. I continued to prepare for the moment facing me.

Concentrating on sobriety helped. Thinking sober is effective for brief periods if the concentration is deep enough. And speaking. I needed to speak to experience the ability to do it clearly and unhesitatingly. I imagined Arline approaching, and spoke out loud. No one paid attention to me and my efforts. I told "her" the day had been a good one and that I had some special news to report. Her reaction was questioning—so I repeated the statement with greater ease and improved diction. It didn't help my inner feeling of impending calamity. My rehearsal ended abruptly. The real Arline was walking toward me.

Each time we meet, the moment of recognition is tender, and thoughtful of the other's well-being. Eighteen years of marriage has not lessened this initial thrill. The years have also made it more difficult for us to hide our feelings or our physical condition. I knew she sensed my plight even from a distance. I read a change in her immediately. Her perception annoyed me. I could not appreciate her attitude when I was not concerned with the amount of alcohol I had drunk.

In concentrating on the coffee, and sobriety, I had lost track of the full effect of my day of controlled drinking. I had "controlled" one half-gallon of white wine, a very large vodka martini in the backyard, two equally large manhattans in the kitchen, three double vodkas at the hotel bar, and three more double vodkas in the past forty-five minutes. Now I wanted to control sobriety. Instantly.

If there remained in my mind any feeling of being in control, it fled like a wounded rabbit. I made a weak suggestion that we stop for a cocktail before the long ride to New Jersey.

"I just want to get home, Fred. That's all—just home. I've had a very tiring day." Her voice trailed, "And now this."

I helped her into the passenger seat, resolved not to tell her the miracle of the day. She will have to wait until our success is certain. When it's a fact, she will be proud. Yes, she will be very proud.

I became very excited about Monday.

*Skid row
alcoholics,
although perhaps
most visible,
comprise fewer
than five percent
of all alcoholics.
The other
ninety-five
percent can be
found in every
walk of life.*
JACK B. WEINER[4]

THE TWENTY-FOUR
DOLLAR ISLAND

"I average twelve drinks a day."

"What time of the day do you begin?"

"At lunch. About 12:30 or a quarter to one."

The doctor thought for a moment. "What time do you go to bed?"

"Normally about eleven. Right after the late news." I tried being honest—very honest about the number of cocktails I averaged in one day. I didn't mention the very late nights of dinner and drinking with out-of-town clients, in-town-clients or just plain drinking. Nor the wine and cognac—only the cocktails. They were drinks.

"Twelve drinks in less than twelve hours is not too much for the kind of business you're in. In fact, if you did not drink a couple at lunch, I'd prescribe a tranquilizer. Since you do drink, and because I consider alcohol nature's tranquilizer, I don't believe it's hurting you." He spoke as though he presented a medical conclusion.

Not trusting what I had just heard, and delighted I had

heard it from the mouth of the doctor who performed this latest physical examination, I jolted upright on the table and spoke with laughter punctuating my words. "Doctor, I know a number of guys sitting in P. J. Moriarity's right now who have been looking all over for you. What a great relief this is!"

"Don't misunderstand what I've just said. And don't overdo it either." He pierced my frivolity with measured words. "I know the pressures of Madison Avenue and its advertising slaughter. Your field of television filming has got to be equally pressured."

"It's much worse," I assured him. I felt as if a license to steal was being issued.

"As long as we see you do not have an ulcer—but seem bent on developing one—and because I feel we can control your blood pressure through weight loss, we don't have to take you off liquor and tobacco at this time. But use some common sense with them," he said, offering me a cigarette and lighting his own. The air in the small examining room soon became filled with our smoke. His endorsement of smoking did not come as a surprise.

He gave my entire life-style an official stamp of approval. I hoped for something to take with me as proof of his findings. An accredited document with all sorts of stamps and seals affixed. If not that, perhaps a letter addressed to all bartenders in New York and New Jersey. Or, a note to Arline would do just fine. I settled for his verbal endorsement and left to report this good fortune to my business colleagues gathering for our daily expense-account business lunch.

While paying the cab driver for the return trip to midtown Manhattan, I remembered this was going to be the first day of reduced drinking. So be it. I'll take it easy. I also recalled today's lunch date was Don Andrews, one of the heaviest drinkers in advertising.

The hatcheck girl took my black cashmere topcoat and handed me a large manila envelope in exchange for my hat.

The size and shape of the envelope told me it contained scripts and storyboards on a job to be bid. New business. My spirits soared.

At the same time my favorite bartender, who had seen me enter, was mixing different spirits. On them I would also soar—and crash. He stabbed noisily at the ice in the glass cocktail mixer, vigorously stirring the martini he knew I would order. While I was greeting my luncheon guest, the frosty long-stemmed glass was placed on a cocktail napkin in front of me. Lemon peel was first squeezed of its citric acid, then gently rubbed around the top of the glass to flavor the first sips. It helps at the beginning. Following that, the vodka or gin takes over and deadens the taste buds and the pain inside. It's during these first moments of drinking that my stomach feels as though someone stabs me with a red-hot poker.

That morning's physical examination didn't reveal an ulcer—but stomach pains persisted from early morning until the time each day when I forced down the first two drinks. Alcohol deadens the pain eventually.

I told our family physician about these pains. He prescribed Gelusil tablets, which I had been eating like peanuts. They give only minor relief. Milk does a better job—but strong drink gives relief as long as I continue drinking. Since I've never been able to get drunk on milk, I'd chosen alcohol as my painkiller.

Cigarettes also taste better with booze. Inhaled on an empty stomach, however, smoke causes considerable pain which I tried to abate with black coffee. Raw stomach walls do not take too kindly to cigarettes and caffeine. I learned that the hard way, which is the way I learn everything.

"To your health, Don," I said with raised martini. The click of our two glasses signaled the start of another ordinary working lunch. Thousands throughout this great city were beginning with the same ritual.

Don's face looked flushed and red. His eyes stared into his drink. Through the smile on his face—but not in his voice—he said, "Sure hope my heart starts with this one." His body shuddered, his head shook, he swallowed deeply and pounded his chest. The first shock passed and we laughed at our misery.

Pointing to the manila envelope, now on the bar, I said, "Thank you for the gift. If you wanted to be anonymous about it, you shouldn't have used an agency envelope."

He was proud of how cleverly the scripts and storyboards were given me. "Since you're buying lunch, I just thought it would be nice to help pay for it." We laughed again and called Tim for another round.

"Pat Johnson, the copywriter on this job, is here from Chicago today. I invited him to join us. Okay with you?" Don asked.

Don is a professional. He knows the film business almost as well as he knows how to get himself and anyone else a free lunch.

The technique is in knowing enough film production reps with whom one's company is presently bidding a job, shooting a job, finishing a job, thinking about bidding a future job, or simply asking to be brought up to date on what that rep's company has been doing. If the agency producer calling happens to be one of who I know likes to drink, he doesn't have to come up with a reason for lunch. I'll find one for him. My excuse for drinking is being with clients who drink. The rationale is that one never knows when one of these characters will have business to give out. I could never be accused of missing these opportunities.

It was impossible for me to object to another member of his agency joining us. It would also be very poor selling for me to protest. I know when I get an opportunity to influence copywriters, art directors, and producers during the initial stages of bidding, we usually are awarded the job. I welcomed the additional voice and hoped he would want to spend this first hour at the bar.

Some clients ask to eat immediately upon entering a restaurant. I don't invite that kind to lunch unless absolutely necessary. They can make an hour and a half seem like two weeks. How boring! Pat Johnson was not boring.

He stormed into the restaurant without removing his overcoat or hat. His scarf dragged across the floor to keep up with its charging owner from Chicago. He stopped short of hitting the bar.

"I was on the phone. They haven't gone to lunch yet back there. What are you guys drinking? You must be Fred Foster. I'm Pat Johnson. Hi."

In unison Don and I said, "Vodka." I added, "Hi."

Tim had come from the other end of the bar.

"I'll have what they're drinking," Pat announced.

I liked the way this lunch was progressing. The increased business phase of Saturday's threefold plan came to mind, and I rewarded myself with another drink. My two guests followed my lead.

"Do you have the storyboards, Fred?" Pat asked.

"Right there." I pointed to the back of the bar where Tim had put the envelope for dry keeping.

"Who do you think should direct them?" The hatcheck girl came and took his wraps.

"I don't know. I haven't seen the boards yet. What's the product?" I asked.

Don spoke. More carefully now. "A new dry cereal. Going into test markets first."

"These aren't test commercials, are they?" I pleaded.

"No," Pat asserted. "We're going full bore on these. The client has approved going national—network prime-time."

"Great," I said. Then, "Let me look them over first and I'll come up with a recommendation on which of our directors would be right for you."

"I've already decided on Hath," Don ventured.

"We'll make that decision in Chicago, Fred." Mr. Pat Johnson of Chicago, Illinois, had just told me who was boss. It wasn't Don, but I had to somehow defend his decision without losing the edge in bidding.

"Don may be right, though," I said. "But first, let's have

one more before our table's ready." They accepted the challenge. I wondered if our friend from the midwest was a belligerent drunk. Don did not look as though he had won the point. He hadn't.

"What's wrong with Ben?" Pat asked. "I like what he did for Pepsi."

"If this is another Pepsi, Ben is probably the director for it." I looked at Don and continued, "Our table's ready. Grab your drinks and we'll drown a steak with them. And then when I've looked the boards over I can tell more about who I think should direct these spots."

I led the way to the dining room, certain our table would be in a choice location, and that the bar check would soon follow. I wanted to be as certain about the outcome of this lunch. I wasn't. Pat Johnson was playing his power role to the hilt and Don was drinking too much.

"The shrimp cocktail, sirloin steak, rare, and some chopped spinach for me, Paul." Our table captain nodded as he wrote, "I'm staying off the potatoes, bread, and fat foods," I boasted. As Don ordered his lunch I interrupted. "Excuse me for a second, guys. I just spotted a friend I must say hello to. Be right back." The cavalry had arrived.

Two weeks before we had completed the production of four thirty-second commercials for a national beer account. The commercials, or spots, as we refer to them, were directed by Hath Calloway—the man Don and I were trying to sell to "Mr. Chicago." The photography turned out to be superb, and the manner in which Hath had directed the multiple talent scenes was a stroke of genius. Everyone involved in the production, hundreds of people, identified themselves proudly and claimed credit for the success—even the messengers who delivered so much as a piece of artwork. We became possessive, referring to the spots as "my beer spots," or "my coke spots," whenever they were mentioned. Not so with a failure. Fiascos appear to have been done by no more than two or three people, all of whom are referred to as "they." And "they" use their authority to make decisions without possessing any creative knowledge or experience relative to advertising or film production. If "they" had not been involved, things would have turned out better. Tony Bellusi was not a "they." He was this week's winner.

"Welcome back, Tony." I extended my open hand. "Here to finish editing?"

"I thought I might find you here. Yeah, I'm back to do the announcer track and put them into release printing as soon as we can. The air date's only three weeks off."

"How are they going over?" I asked the question because I needed the praise I felt coming.

"The boys at the brewery told us these are the best commercials ever done for them. And probably the best ever produced in the industry." He spoke with pride, like a new father, and took more credit for the birth than he deserved. Typically, Tony had not had to carry much during the development of the commericals, and had arrived on the scene when birth was imminent. Now he claimed parenthood. That was all right with me—I just wanted him to repeat the successful outcome to my other guests.

"They're the best we've ever produced," I echoed, "and I'll bet they'll win awards all over the country. Are you alone?"

"Yes. And as I said before, I thought I might find you here since I need someone for lunch."

"Great. Come and join us. I'm with Don Andrews. You know Don. He's got a copywriter from Chicago with him."

"If you're sure I won't be interfering." He didn't mean it.

"Not at all. Tim, put Tony's drink on my tab—and hold onto it. We'll be back for cordials."

On the way back to the table I briefed Tony on what we were doing. "So, don't be afraid to mention your success with Hath," I coached.

The arrival of a fresh body demanded we delay our eating while he had a drink before lunch. I ordered a new round for the table. No one objected. Tony's presence effectively stopped all conversation about who was making decisions on the new breakfast cereal bid. Don's self-worth hung on.

Four shrimp cocktails, four sirloin steaks, and two full bottles of Beaujolais 1969 vanished during insignificant conversation and much service rendered by two efficient waiters. I related the good news of the morning's medical examination and suggested coffee and cognac back at the bar. No objections. We were following doctor's orders.

Standing at a bar with clients is the arena in which I am most comfortable—and the most victorious. It is here that I score well. When men are drinking heavily, and not spending their own money, they feel obligated to contribute information connected with present or future productions in their shops. I promote the atmosphere in which they more freely talk about these matters by mixing ad agencies with alcohol. I usually do not have lunch or drinks with only one person, and I ordinarily invite producers from various agencies at the same time. Then I lay the groundwork. Today's objective was to convince our Chicago visitor that Hath Calloway was the only man in the world capable of directing his breakfast food commercials. It was a stroke of luck that Tony had arrived while I was pitted against one company. Now I could maneuver.

I spoke to Pat Johnson while looking at Tony. "Tony has just finished a shoot with Hath. Haven't you, Tony?" I stepped back to order the cordials and continue my role as host. And to listen intently.

Tony earned his lunch admirably. He spoke first of the creative concept within the story line of the spots, and then of his function as the producer who came in and actually put the production together. He left no doubt that he was the savior on the job. I thought he would never get to the good part. Us.

"I'm glad I insisted on Hath Calloway. Here is a talent. I gotta tell ya, here is a talent." He asked for another Stinger (imported cognac and imported white Creme de Menthe, a drink which gives the effect of brushing the teeth while getting high). "He was beautiful. He added camera angles and shots we never thought of during prep time. And the crew. Hath had them busting themselves for him. That's the kind of guy he is. Crews love to work for him. Your price was a little high, Fred, but Hath made it all worthwhile."

"I used him on the Duncan Hines thing we shot in Florida," Don said. He could barely talk now. The day's intake of liquor showed clearly. "Oh, you wouldn't know about that one, Pat. It's not in your group." Too much had been said by Don, and he knew it. He sat lower.

"I know about it, Don. But I didn't know Hath had done it. That's all. I know everything else about it," he slurred. Everyone showed signs of being drunk.

I knew I was okay. Sober by a narrow margin perhaps, but sober and on top of these guys. Don always drank more than he could handle. Every time I was with him he got sloppy drunk, and helped me to believe I was not the one with the drinking problem.

Tony demanded more time. He didn't want these two to pass so lightly over his significant contribution to influencing the American public in the brand of beer they would soon drink generously. He got off his bar stool. Standing between them he could thus speak down to within inches of their ears. His were the loudest and most audible secrets ever told.

"Because of these commercials we are going to be able to raise our client's advertising budget for beer by another million dollars. What do you think of that?" Without waiting for an answer, he continued, "And I'm the guy already picked to shoot the next four spots in January." He stood tall and proud, holding on to the bar for support.

I would not forget four new commercials coming up in January. Pat Johnson turned and sat stiffly upright.

"Our creative review board is about to approve a completely new national campaign for Pepsi. It's going to be a big one, too. We're thinking of shooting in Norway, Sweden, Denmark and all over the Continent."

That was Pat's best shot. He scored a touchdown. It stunned Tony because he knew the immensity of other Pepsi television campaigns. His agency did not claim possession of a client so generous with their ad budgets.

I caught the shot Pat threw, and would not forget the additional Pepsi production coming soon. December and January looked good for us. It all seemed so easy. Success is only a matter of time. My friend euphoria arrived. "Where were you Saturday night when I needed you?" I whispered.

"What was that you said?" Pat asked.

Without missing the pace of conversation, I responded quickly, "Could we get out of here. I've got to get busy on your bid, and as soon as I've looked the boards over I'll be able to suggest a director for you."

Don wanted to know how soon I could have the bid finished. It was too early in the match to respond to that query.

I answered the question with a question. "How long are you going to be in town, Pat?"

"I have a three-thirty out of LaGuardia tomorrow."

I asked Don when he needed the bids in. He looked at Pat silently.

I jumped in without delay. "Why don't I come up to your office about eleven? We can go over everything, you can give me your creative input, and I can show you our latest reel before we go to lunch."

Don came to life. "Lunch would be great. What time?"

He was ignored by all of us as Pat confirmed the eleven o'clock meeting for tomorrow. All drinks on the bar were consumed in one greedy swallow. I turned to watch them leave, fumbling in pockets for tip money with which to "purchase" their coats. Tony stayed behind as I signed all bar and lunch checks. The owner loves me. I spend between nine hundred and a thousand dollars each month in this one restaurant. I also write over one hundred and fifty thousand dollars worth of new film production orders each month—in this one restaurant. It's cheap money I'm spending. And not mine. We put enough funds in each budget to buy lunches and dinners for our out-of-town guests, and since we mark up the budget costs, we actually make a profit on each steak. I thanked Tony for the lunch.

"Don't thank me. You're the one who's signing checks," he laughed.

"Tony, you were great. Thanks then for the support. If I can't thank you for the lunch, I can certainly thank you for support. How about a drink tonight before I split for the suburbs?"

"You don't have to do that, Fred. Go on home to your family if you'd like."

My arm went over his shoulder as we walked out. Liquor makes for strange bedfellows, and I extended the invitation again. The cold air of Fifty-fourth Street felt good. I issued an order this time. "I'll see you at six in the bar of the Four Seasons and miss the heavy part of traffic before heading home." He accepted. I had another date with a client. It was also another date with trouble.

Tony left for his recording session. I turned towards Park Avenue, headed for the Post Office building on Third, where I set up temporary office space away from the studio. The Post Office has a large bank of public telephones, and postal clerks behind modern cages where dimes for phone calls can be easily obtained. It's very convenient, and also very smart not to return to work after lunch in this profession. Everyone knows ours is a drinking business, but intoxication is not welcomed during daylight hours. The telephone does not reveal my breath, my stagger, or my skin tone. It helps disguise my speech. I sound more sober. Welcomed. I dialed the studio to report in.

Good news overflowed. We had just been awarded the filming of six commercials from another Chicago agency. This came as the result of my trip there last month, so full credit showered upon me. I laid my luncheon prosperity upon them and was rewarded with increased accolades and unspoken permission to take the rest of the day off. I promised an afternoon of calling on more agencies and agreed to a breakfast meeting regarding the cereal bid from Don Andrews. I would also use that breakfast encounter as the occasion to seek a pay raise. I needed it to begin saving and for building an investment portfolio which would surely surprise and please my family. Saturday's dreams were coming true and the bonus was the green light from the company doctor.

A quick call to Arline brought mixed reactions. She registered pleasure from my selling accomplishments but a very cold acceptance of my cocktail date at six. I assured her it would not be a late night. I did not tell her of my drinking license.

Another call. My P & G client will meet me at P. J. Clark's in ten minutes. He can have a drink before getting back across the street to work. Good. Now I need one more drinking customer to fill in the late afternoon. The producer of a large airline account will meet me at five. He's good for one or two before dashing madly for Grand Central Station and Connecticut. This "sales" schedule will take me to six o'clock and I won't be drinking alone. Alcoholics drink alone. Successful businessmen drink with clients. In nice surroundings.

P. J. Clark's had recently become a popular meeting haunt for the advertising crowd now occupying several new office buildings on Third Avenue. The Third Avenue "L" was taken down in the first step to revitalizing Manhattan's East Side. Then the buildings went up, from Forty-eighth Street north to Fifty-sixth Street, and Madison Avenue had competition for advertising agency tenants. The local gin mills along the avenue thrived. Some bars were demolished to make way for the skyscrapers, but one in particular fought and won its right to remain.

P. J. Clark's, renowned as the saloon in which the movie *The Lost Weekend* had been filmed, was able to defy the bulldozer. It now stands alone, surrounded by towering steel and glass, as a reminder that Ray Milland roamed these streets in search of bottles he had hidden. The neighborhood was then a part of skid row. Drunken derelicts wandered over and slept upon these sidewalks and alleys. I never forgot that film. But I never identified with it.

Successful businessmen do not hide bottles or sleep in Third Avenue alleys. We use expense accounts and credit cards.

*"He who
rides a tiger
is afraid to
dismount"*
CHINESE PROVERB

RIDING THE TIGER

The 7:05 A.M. bus to New York splashed and hissed to a stop. The monster was conspicuously disagreeable that I had interrupted its early morning dash to Manhattan on this rain-soaked October morning. Its spasmodic windshield wipers threw ice water at my uncovered head. I would have felt less timid if others were boarding with me. Its driver, a machine within a machine, took the commuter ticket I presented, punched a hole in it, hissed the door closed, and pressed the accelerator pedal full to the floor, all in one fluid motion.

We shot out in pursuit of the time lost in picking me up. I wasn't prepared for the sudden forward movement. With complete disregard for my comfort or safety, the machine at the wheel caused me to fall into a nearby seat, where my body caught up with the speeding bus. I looked into his enormous rear-view mirror as our eyes met. He smiled. I didn't—last night remained too vivid.

I had dropped off Tony Bellusi, my beer client of recent

success, at his hotel about two-thirty this morning. The cab ride home only took thirty minutes, and I was in bed no later than three. Arline was not in bed with me when the alarm buzzed me to consciousness an hour before. Three hours sleep had made it a very short night, and the rejection I felt from my spouse made me want to flee into work. I had remembered the breakfast meeting promise, and broken the drink promise. Today will be different. Yesterday was not my fault. I should have ended the evening after my fourth martini with Tony at the Four Seasons cocktail lounge. Instead, I suggested one of the city's most celebrated west-side Italian restaurants. Tony could not resist. I convinced him the little Italian lady who did the cooking would remind him of his mother, and that the restaurant was on my route home. I had invented the narrative about the cook, and although the journey to New Jersey had been shortened, my immediate needs would be served only if I stayed in New York. If Tony abandoned me now, I would lose my rationale for guilt-free drinking. At ten-thirty we sat down to eat, but not before I dutifully called home.

"Mother isn't here, Dad," Ann reported. "She's gone to a meeting with Mrs. Hancock." Her voice was impersonal.

Relief came because I did not have to explain why I wasn't home. Or at least on my way home. "I'm having dinner with Chicago clients. Tell mother I'll be home in a few hours."

"OK. Bye." She hung up.

I felt uneasy—as though I had been speaking to a telephone operator. I missed being verbally lashed. Misunderstood. Ann's report upset me. It's an inappropriate response to a working husband's loving call. When the home front doesn't care—when she's not even there—a loss is felt. Some of the fun is taken from drinking. But not all of it. I knew that this morning.

Jostling back to Manhattan gave me time to remember how I felt last night. To what kind of meeting did Arline go?

Why Betty Hancock? She and Arline have little in common. They rarely see each other as far as I know, and I certainly do not associate with Tom Hancock, a raving alcoholic who hasn't worked for years. He has been in and out of institutions because of drinking, and has seen the inside of several jails. Everyone in town knows about poor Tom and what he's done to his family. Betty's income as a dental technician keeps the family alive. I have little respect for a man who lets himself go, and then won't do anything to improve his condition. If Arline was near that drunkard last night, I'm safe. She'll feel better about our marriage.

From my point of view, our marriage is exceptional. I have always loved Arline. I'm proud to be the provider of my fine family. It would please me if she drank more so I wouldn't feel as guilty about my own. And I would be delighted if she became more active in golf. Other than for these minor annoyances, I'm perfectly happy with the mother of my two children. When Arline enters any gathering, she is consistently the most beautiful female present. I'm a most proud husband, and equally proud father when our children are with us.

Ann and Ken may be overindulged suburban teenagers, but I believe they are more mature, more well-behaved, and more intelligent than their peers. I enjoy their personalities. They're fun. We four take pleasure in our style of entertaining, travel, dress, and vacations, things not found in most families we know. Outwardly we are a storybook, Walt Disney family. We even go to church.

I'm a Presbyterian elder. They gave me the complete package with the office, ordination included. It was the first time I could remember being on my knees in church. Soon after, I gave the principal talk in a Layman's Sunday service. From the pulpit. It was almost a sermon. People told me they liked what I said. I felt holy greeting parishioners at the door as they left church. Important. And hung over from Saturday night. A drink would have helped before that little act, but Sunday morning didn't fit into my drinking pattern. I still had control. I could do it my way.

"Those who center upon themselves and have their way, don't like their way; they do as they like, and then don't like what they do; they express themselves, and then find the self that is expressed souring on their hands."[5] Thus wrote E. Stanley Jones, years before I could receive his wisdom.

Roy L. Smith adds another dimension: "It has been said by some wit that the man who is wrapped up in himself makes a very small package."[6]

I may be wrapped completely in myself—and Smith is probably correct—I make a very small package. But not to me. Everything I have ever attempted in life I have attained, through hard work and clever manipulating. In my obsession to succeed in New York City, I am, of course, centering upon myself. I see no other way to continue our life-style. I'm the one who must do it, and since I know how to do it, I see no reason to ask questions of anyone. I have the answers. Now, all I must do is follow the course I've set. This breakfast with Sidney Steen is key. As the cab carried me through the rain-swept garment district, I had no way of knowing which obsession, success or drink, would be nourished. My breakfast colleague knew.

Sid is the third partner, along with our two film directors, Hath Calloway and Ben Kaufman. Sid came in with the money as the two young talents were emerging. He abandoned his very lucrative law practice for the role of business manager of the fledgling studio and transformed the young company into the most aggressive and viable enterprise in the national advertising community. My sales have been a major contributor to this growth, and are responsible for the winning hand I hold in this game. To lose my services at this juncture would certainly be a setback. I thought.

"I've hired a new salesman." He trumped my ace!

The bacon hardened in my capsized stomach. The pay raise vanished. Fantasized company stock tumbled. Self-esteem fled. The seed of panic broke ground. I watered it with coffee. The St. George Hotel snack bar is not a pleasant atmosphere in which to receive good news. For bad news it's terrifying. With an October rain, it's a funeral home. Am I witnessing my own burial rites?

"Who did you hire?" I asked. I could not bring myself to ask, "Why?"

"You don't know him. He's new to the business. A lawyer I know from practice. Hath and Ben think he'll be great."

Sid looked deeply into my head. He was not asking my approval. My business card contains the title of Sales Manager, but we all know it's to impress the Midwest clientele. Not to manage a sales department.

In icy monotone he continued, "We want you to work with him. Take him on calls with you. Show him around the town."

Insecurity shook me. "Don't you think I'm keeping the boys busy enough?" I yelled. The volume of business I bring in demanded an affirmative reply to my weighted question.

"You're not covering all the agencies. We're missing too many of them because you don't move around enough. Your circle of new business is not widening because you stay with the same ones all the time. I want more than that from this city." He spoke as a judge and passed sentence from his bench of wealth and supreme self-confidence.

"It has taken me years to develop these guys, Sid. And they certainly keep coming through for me." It was a weak defense which did not fill the daily afternoons of drinking. "But I'll be glad to show him around if that's what you want. Between the two of us hitting this town, we'll have your two partners working nights and weekends." I attempted teamwork in exchange for being substituted. I wondered if the new man drank.

"I'll introduce you this morning," he said. "Let's have lunch in my office. We'll run down the agency list and set up some assignments."

Have lunch in his office! I can see it now. Soggy sandwiches from the Stage Delicatessen. Just what I need for this stomach of mine. "I won't be able to today, Sid. I have an eleven o'clock with Don Andrews. We're going over these boards with Pat Johnson before he goes back to Chicago, and I've committed to lunch with them."

Sid squeezed some grapefruit juice my way, and without looking up, declared, "Two days in a row with those guys. Looks like overkill to me. So we'll meet in my office right after we leave here." I had my marching orders. He paid the bill and we walked to the studio without a word passing between us.

The studio reception room instantly became wall-to-wall white. Thirty to forty sets of perfect white teeth sparkled at us as we entered. Behind the sets of teeth were the same number of beautiful young and happy women, radiating instant joy, health, youth, and every-ready smiles. No one was sad. I brilliantly deduced that a casting session for a toothpaste commercial must be in progress. The room full of teeth didn't know who we were, so they paraded as though someone opened venetian blinds on the back wall. The energy these young ladies discharged at nine o'clock annoyed our receptionist. She had just spent over an hour on the subway coming from her home in the upper Bronx, and arrived worn out. We didn't see her teeth too often.

"Good morning, Annie," I offered. Sid had silently picked up his phone messages enroute to his office. Annie took another call. The venetian blind of teeth closed. I thought the room became a little darker. Annie winked good-bye. I turned into the hall leading to my office.

"I still haven't got your expense account, Foster," reverberated from the recesses of our accounting department. "And I'm not giving you another cent until you're up to date. I mean it." Pearl Donchey, our accountant, had offered her morning greeting, and the entire staff knew I had arrived. Waiting in my office was an unexpected visitor who also knew I would appear momentarily.

The long white hall past accounting led to my office. Arline had done the decorating a year ago, and the used-brick wall behind the huge oak desk Sid Steen had loaned me from his law office created an atmosphere of solidarity and good taste which always pleased me. I expected this morning to be no different. Then I saw Lenny Schaeffer.

"What in the world are you doing here, Len?"

He looked perplexed. "You're kidding me."

"No, I'm not kidding you. I really didn't know you were coming to town. What's the occasion?"

"What's the occasion? Now I know you're not serious. You're too much, Fred. You knew I was due in on a shoot. Who do you think the casting session is for?"

"I thought I recognized your teeth in the reception room," I joked. I moved around to my side of the desk, and while hanging my coat on the tall antique rack Arline found, I speculated how this could happen without my knowledge. My mind raced for an explanation. I could not forget a job from Len Schaeffer. He's one of my major sales triumphs for this company. Two years ago, St. Louis, Missouri, except for my in-laws, didn't know this company existed. I'm the guy who opened the market for us. We've shot pet food, beer, and previous toothpaste commericals for Len. He's been good for $250,000 annually. I wouldn't have forgotten this production. I did forget to cover myself from Sid Steen, though.

"Sid gave you the bid on this one, didn't he?"

"Yes, it was early last week. He told me you were out of town."

Not so. I have been in town for the past four weeks. Why would Sid keep this sale from me? Fear and guilt joined the panic I had for breakfast. But it was now time to put up the good front in the presence of a client. To keep peace and maintain outward company harmony so Lenny would only see us as a group he could trust. He has come to us to solve his problems—not to become involved in ours.

"Now I remember," I lied. "I was on the coast. Sid did mention he opened a package of storyboards and scripts from you. I was so involved in the shoot and the weather out there, I just forgot about your job and never did ask your schedule. Later on I was told we were working with you again, and now that you're here, it's great, Len. Did you bring Madeline?"

The ease with which I changed courses pleased me. It pleased Len, also, for it led into his next concern.

"When you were in St. Louis, you told me to bring her with me on the next job, Fred. And that I didn't have to worry about any of it." He searched for financial relief. I offered it.

"And that's exactly right, my friend. You don't. Let me take care of the week for you and Madeline. Now, where are you staying and what are your plans?" I should not have asked. He and his wife go first class.

Before I had the chance to order coffee for us, I learned they were at the Pierre Hotel. At $125 a night. I had recommended it, he said. He then informed me they were looking forward to seeing, *Hello, Dolly*, the current Broadway hit musical. I had promised tickets to it any time he was in New York. I didn't promise him we would go. Arline and I have seen this show twice. Three times is too much, even for a good client. On another occasion we did see one show three times. I felt certain I could understudy the leading man if he suddenly had a heart attack. And if I had not had that last martini before the show began.

"Arline and I have seen that one, Len. Suppose I set you up with tickets? You can pick them up at the box office Thursday night. We'll have dinner with you, and drop you at the theater before heading home. Where would you like to have dinner?" I dared ask.

Len had promised his wife the "21 Club," which is the most prestigious, and expensive, restaurant in New York City. I don't recall suggesting that one. It must have been during lunch in St. Louis. Midwest martinis cause me to make weird suggestions. Or is it the clean air out there? I'm convinced I think better with carbon monoxide in me.

His choice of restaurants was fine with me. It doesn't

make any difference where I eat. I grade the choice by the bar, and the "21" has a great bar. "When does your production meeting begin?" I asked.

"Right now. I'm waiting for someone to direct me," he replied.

"Okay. We'll get you started, then how about meeting me for lunch?"

"The New York Athletic Club?" he asked. Len is not bashful. I wondered how elegantly they live in St. Louis. On his salary.

"Sure, that's a great idea, but no gambling on the pool. You're too good for me."

He laughed his victor's laugh. I laughed with him because I knew I could now manipulate him for the next job. The one he's doing now was last week's sale. It's about to be charged for at least eight hundred dollars in client entertainment, including money I lose shooting pool in the billiard room of the plush New York Athletic Club.

"I assume, Len, that you do want to engage in a little pool playing during lunch."

"It's the only reason I use you guys for production. You don't think I come here for talent, do you?" He loved his own humor. I laughed—but only to establish his statement as a joke. In his head, not mine.

Our public address system announced the call to his production meeting. As Len set off for the call, he promised to be in the billiard room not later than twelve-thirty. "I know the way, Fred. Just don't forget to tell the man at the door I'm coming." Lunch is getting complicated, and swiftly growing in numbers. Today St. Louis and Chicago will meet in competition with long wooden sticks with green felt tips. They will eat, drink, and be merry. I will eat and drink. My secretary must help me. I buzzed.

"I know Sid wants me in his office, but you've got to help me with reservations." I said. "Len Schaeffer brought his wife with him. Get me two tickets for *Dolly* in his name at the box office. Thursday. Then I need four at the '21,' same night. About seven o'clock, so they can make their curtain and still have time for dinner. Call the A.C. and reserve a pool table for four of us at twelve-thirty. That's today. We'll be there for lunch. Make sure the front desk has Len's name as well as Don Andrews and Pat Johnson. Arline and I will have to take Len and Madeline to dinner tonight, so get me four at the Homestead. Eight o'clock will be fine for that one. Then we'll take them to the Village and hope they get lost. I should be so lucky."

"Slow down, Fred," she pleaded. "You're wound up so tight, and it's not even ten o'clock. Here, drink some coffee and sit."

"Okay, but get me a hundred from Pearl. Tell her expense accounts come after client needs. You know how to handle her." I smiled. She threw up her hands and turned to go.

"Wait till you meet the new rep," she tossed.

"What's his name?" I still could not ask, "Why."

"Dave Bartel."

"Where in the world did they dig him up?" I calmly questioned.

"Don't ask me," she replied. "All I know is that he's a friend of Sid's, and that the three of them have been meeting for weeks. They stay late and laugh a lot." She left my office, and me to ponder.

They had to be laughing at me, about me, or because of what was going to happen to me. There can be no other explanation. I began to feel uncomfortable. The room, and the entire studio, felt hostile. Guilt for not being here after lunch most days, and never after four o'clock, swept in. I must spend more time with those three, even though I'm not at ease in their presence. I feel I'm their target.

Years later I will know how easily I'm manipulated by these men. A *Los Angeles Times* article, written by an alcoholism counselor I would come to value as a friend, spoke directly to me. Peggy Irwin wrote, "Alcoholics possess a passive-aggressive personality, the traits of which include

being hypercritical, very judgmental, resentful of authority, yet desperately in search of approval because they have
no self-approval, and they are perfectionists, but lack balance. Further, they are either over-achievers or under-
achievers, and many are unable to take stress, yet gravitate
toward stressful jobs." Peggy must have known my boss. Or
the new rep.

Dave Bartel stood up as I entered Sid's crowded office.
My fear of being replaced vanished. The young man standing before me, stroking his Groucho Marx mustache, will
never make it with the agency producers I know. They'll
laugh him right out of lunch before he has his first drink.
And, if he doesn't drink, he's not even in the game. Believe
me.

"Dave will call on all the nondrinking producers."

That's not what Sid announced. It's how it sounded to
me, for the list they had prepared did not contain one
personable client. Most of them were new in the
industry—and younger. I had heard of many, but never
called on them. I can't cover the world. Particularly that
part which only takes one hour for lunch. How dull. I had
to get out of this meeting and away from these two. But first
I'll show Dave how this outfit honors sales territories.

"Why didn't you tell me we were shooting for Schaeffer?"
I challenged. "The least you can do is let me know when my
clients are coming. It was really embarrassing to find Len
in my office just now."

"No one owns clients around here. They all belong to the
company. What difference does it make who brings in the
business, as long as it comes in?" He didn't apologize. He
looked at Dave Bartel as he spoke. I felt invisible.

"Sid, he sent me the storyboards and scripts for bidding.
Are you opening my mail now?"

He turned to me. "All mail goes through Pearl. She
opens everything addressed to the company regardless of
whose name is on it. Suppose you were away? Or sick?"

"I was neither away nor sick, Sid. I was right here." I

looked at Dave during this parry. His reaction was neutral.

"You may have been in the city, but you were not *right here* most of the time. I can never find you when I need you, so I got the bid in and out. Besides, Len and I get along just fine. We're having dinner tomorrow with them." He looked at Dave during that proclamation. I had no defense for absenteeism. I looked for an escape.

"Okay, Sid. You two pick whoever you want Dave to call on. I'll help you any way I can, Dave." I retreated towards the door. "But for now I must get over to Don Andrews' office. I'll check with you after lunch."

In the privacy of my own office, I called Arline. She agreed to meet at Toots Shor's after work, and would join us for dinner. She didn't question my lunch plans today. Why? She usually questions my lunch plans, and comments on the drinking behavior of the men involved. Recently she stopped the inquisitions. I felt an uncomfortable freedom, born of pleasure for not requiring a defense, and concern that she is no longer interested in my daily agenda. I don't know how to react to this new attitude except to ignore it. I'll bury this episode in the same cellar I've put many earlier guilts and pretend nothing is changing. Thank God for clients. They're necessary to the success of this sham. If they drink.

At eleven-thirty I walked out of Don's office, only two crosstown blocks from the athletic club. I now have, and understand, all the specifications of the new breakfast cereal commercials. My estimate to do the filming is $120,000. The price did not frighten them, so I converted the conversation from the conditional "if" we shoot, to the more positive "when" we shoot. Before leaving, we established tentative schedules, which I reported to the studio by phone from their office. And in their presence. It's important they know we're reserving time for their job prior to actually being awarded the project. Putting a "hold" on a film director makes it more difficult for them to give the assignment to a competitor. I had made it tough for them to say no to our bid—and easy to say yes to lunch. They will meet us at twelve-thirty. I felt in control.

Could our new man negotiate with such boldness? Never! Why then, am I fearful in the wake of this fresh victory? I would find some answers on Fifty-ninth Street, and without thought, seek my natural state of con- sciousness—mildly drunk. A cunning, baffling, and power- ful disease bid for control of my fears. It was the highest bid submitted. I awarded my life to its power. Anxiously.

The New York Athletic Club lies in the path of many of New York's most enjoyable cocktail lounges. Fifty-ninth Street is a mecca of sophisticated, proper, and expensive small hotels. Each has its own atmosphere in which to drink and large windows through which one can watch the herds of people walking the avenue. I chose a vantage point allow- ing the broadest view of foot traffic. In forty-five minutes I'm due in the billiard room, now only doors away. But not before I'm ready.

Don Andrews and his Chicago superior will follow my route to lunch. They will pass this observation post. I will see them and quickly finish the current martini, pay the check, and leave for our appointed date. I will be only moments late, as though rushing from another ad agency, and now graciously give to them three hours of my ex- tremely busy day. We successful businessmen are con- stantly in demand. So are some cocktail waitresses.

The scenario was performed as written. Halfway through my third drink, my cue to exit appeared. My two clients braced their bodies against the dampness and wind. Pat Johnson carried his overnight bag. He would leave for Chicago directly from here. His day of work completed, lunch will be a party before the flight. I love parties and feel good about going to this one. I didn't like my weakness for having three gin martinis so quickly and thus failing in my promise to drink only wine during lunch. The breakfast with Sid, and the new salesman surprise, were each reason enough to seek escape. I'll begin the new drinking program tomorrow. That makes more sense than to attempt moderation today. Especially while playing pool.

"It's almost two o'clock. Doesn't anyone want to eat lunch?" asked Len Schaeffer. He pushed two full scotches aside, unable to drink them on an empty stomach. "I can't keep up with you guys," he complained.

"Len, if you can't drink, don't come to lunch," laughed Don Andrews.

We all laughed with him. Len and Don had quickly become good friends and losing pool partners as Pat and I consistantly outpointed them. I used my custom pool cue for the first time. It improved my game and perhaps my ability to drink more without suffering loss of visual depth perception or steady hands. Even after three more martinis. A decision not to return to the studio relieved me of seeing Sid and his new salesman. The need to take Len and his wife to dinner tonight justified this absence. They're hard work. We ordered lunch.

Crabmeat cocktails, club steaks, and cucumber salads appeared between three bottles of wine. Cognac and Grand Marnier Liqueur were dessert. We wisely stayed away from sweets. Additional pots of steaming black coffee tried vainly to restore sobriety. Shooting pool became an effort. The balls appeared smaller. The table became huge—an acre of green. My custom cue no longer fit my fingers. The two attendants serving the room hovered nearby, conspicuously annoyed by our noise, our language, and our misuse of valuable property. After many phone calls, our Chicago guest succeeded in getting a seat on the six o'clock flight. He had missed his three-thirty plane somewhere into his second bourbon old-fashioned cocktail Len remained the only sober man at the party. His move to leave signaled the end of lunch.

"Arline and I will meet you at Toot's around six. We've got reservations in the Village. Dinner at the Homestead. Madeline will love it. Okay?"

"Fine, if you think you're going to be up to it," he answered.

"Of course. I'll be fine. The coffee knows its job, and I've got two more hours of calls to make way over on the east side of town. Let's get out of here," I challenged. To focus on signing the check, I closed one eye and leaned across a covered pool table. Ninety-three dollars for lunch and pool seemed high, but I could not calculate the figures to check accuracy. I trusted the club management to be honest, and signed my number.

Don Andrews almost fell as the swinging door thrust him into the street. I pulled him aside while the other two claimed the emptying taxi at the curb. I worried about Don. Again he had drunk much more than he could handle. He became unable to guide himself.

"Don, you and I are going back in for some steam and a rubdown."

He nodded, "Fine, ole buddy."

Len and Pat waved from their cab. "I'll see you tonight, Fred."

Two hours later Don and I looked almost human again. We had cooked our bodies in the steam room, dried our pores in the hot-dry room, pounded our fragile bodies with high pressure water jets and slept for thirty minutes after the masseur rubbed our bodies with soothing oil and therapeutic hands. Shortly after five we looked great and smelled as if it were eight o'clock in the morning. Even the bartender in the men's grill welcomed us. We had our first martini of the evening. A new life began.

"That was great, Fred. I feel much better now. Boy, those drinks at lunch were powerful." He sipped the first taste without lifting the glass. It's safer this way. No shakes.

"I think we were all up tight with Pat in here. Then Lenny didn't make it any easier with his attitude. You'd think we did this every day—not because he and Pat were visiting," I confessed. "I'm glad they're gone."

"You're going to be okay on the cereal job," Don said.

"I hope so, but how come?"

"Don't give me your final bid until I get the others in. We all want you to do the commercials, so I'll let you know where to be, even though the guess you gave us looks good."

"That's perfect, Don, because Sid has gone and hired another guy to sell and I need all the ammunition I can get to show them how important people like you are to our success."

"Don't let them get to you, Fred. You have too many of us in this town who will be working with you no matter where you're located. We stick together and survive. You're one of the group. Relax." I relaxed.

We each had one more drink and left to go our separate ways. He ran for an early train from Grand Central Station and I took a cab to Toots Shor's on Fifty-second Street. I avoided calling the studio. That proved to be a big mistake.

"Have you spoken with Sid this afternoon?" Arline asked before I sat down.

"No. I've been with clients all afternoon." That was not a lie.

"Well, you'd better call him right now. He called here so I took the call. He said it's important. Is everything all right between you two?"

"Of course. I'm just having scheduling problems—and they're good problems to have. I'll be right back. Order me a scotch and water. You look great tonight." She didn't react.

"Sid, it was not possible for me to call in. I was too busy locking in the Andrews' shoot. It's ours at about a hundred and twenty if we can do it," I expressed.

His telephone voice was happy. "I don't see how we can do it where you've scheduled it. Dave's already filled those dates for Hath. He got his first job in."

"That's impossible, Sid," I claimed. "He may have gotten a bid to do, but there's no way he could get the storyboards and the job in one day, and on his first day in the business. Who does he know?"

"Me," was his frightening answer.

"OK, you're playing games with me. Semantics," I tried. "Or, you're giving him your jobs. The ones you've already got in bid."

"If he's going to be taking over some of my load, I've got to start him out on a positive note. Yes, I am giving him some of mine, but they're still his to produce. He and I booked Hath's time. You called production to schedule and they didn't know we had committed the time."

"What am I supposed to tell Don? He's fighting like crazy for me."

"See if they'll switch directors. Sell them Peter. You can do it."

"Sure I can. You know as well as I do that Peter doesn't have the experience for this kind of dialogue directing. And with kids, yet. How big is Dave's job?"

"Big enough," he stabbed. "See what you can do tomorrow. In the meanwhile, have a nice dinner with Len and his wife. And give my regards to Arline." He hung up.

His words, "if he's going to be taking over some of my load," would not leave me. A prince had been born this day, and he wasn't a prince of peace. Not for me. Not yet.

"Are you all right, Fred?" Arline searched. "You don't look too good."

"I'm fine, hon. It's just that Sid gets in my way. He's not professional in the business. He may be a good businessman and lawyer, but he does not know how the agency boys work. Now he wants me to sell Peter to Don Andrews, and Peter is not only new with us but he's directed only two commercials in his life. These guys are not about to buy a director with that limited experience to shoot a big package of commercials which will determine if a product goes on the national market or not." I stopped to breathe. Arline looked worried.

"Are you sure that doctor told you your blood pressure was under control? Your face is very red."

"It's from the steam room and swimming. I worked out at the club today," I remarked. "I'm fine. It's Sid and the new man he hired."

"Are you going to be looking for work with another studio?" Arline comes immediately to the point. She knows me well.

I delayed answering her question by signaling the waiter. Scotch and water was not doing a thing for me. "I'd like a Canadian Club manhattan, straight up with a dash of bitters and on the sweet side." I looked at Arline's questioning eyes. "No, I'm not looking for another studio, even though I got a call from Tom Halstad last week. I just have to watch myself around these two lawyers who are trying to take over the film industry," I boasted.

Arline didn't respond to my intelligent observation of Sid, nor to my unusual determination to stick with a problem. Not to quit. The offer from the Halstad studio passed unnoticed, and now she ignored the fresh, more potent drink set before me. I feel uneasy again. She is not influenced by what I'm doing. She's in control of herself. I continue to observe the signs of affection in her eyes and in the manner in which she smiles. Her freshly applied perfume tells me she wants to attract. Everything about her is as always, except her self-confidence. Something, or somebody, is changing her responses. Those meetings she's going to came to mind. I felt a confrontation coming. Arline wanted me to question but I was saved again.

Len and his wife Madeline brought our discussion to an end. They were on time. Precisely as the cavalry of yesterday, except here the bad men had retreated, and the settlers were not in danger. This battlefield was quiet, despite the abundance of lethal weapons camouflaged as harmless cocktails.

Introductions were made. We settled in for a few more drinks before proceeding to the Homestead restaurant and dinner. Arline stayed with one tall bourbon and water for the entire drinking period. Madeline requested ice be added three times to her drink. She drinks so slowly, I concluded I spill more than she gets into her stomach. Her obvious distaste for liquor, and penetrating look of condemnation at Len each time he ordered another, effectively muzzled him. He could only squeeze in one during the cocktail hour, and one more before eating. I was very thankful for lunch. Between five-thirty and ten-thirty this evening, I have been able to comfortably order only three before dinner. The wine during our meal helped. I enjoyed the bottle—alone. One double cognac, with coffee, is a terrific dessert, approved by the "Drinking Man's Diet," so, while our guests and Arline chose the standard sweets, I satisfied my need. Until we got home.

The happy-face kitchen clock smiled and pointed to eleven-forty-five. In fifteen minutes it will be tomorrow. Alone in this kitchen is the first time today I have been quiet. Arline is asleep. In our bedroom. I looked up and whispered, "Thank you." Warm cognac swirled in the large brandy snifter cradled in the palm of my cupped hands. Its strong aroma drew me near. I drank and reflected.

This Presbyterian elder has had himself quite a day! Seventeen hours of riding the tiger. Another normal day. The ship's clock in the front hall announced eight bells. Midnight. A new watch begins somewhere at sea. A new future begins for me. I feel it coming. Pride will not allow me to remain. My resentments against Sid will send me fleeing. The new tiger I mount will become the most fearsome in the asphalt wilderness of Manhattan.

But ride him I must.

It has been said that for some people religion is like an artificial limb. It has neither warmth nor life; and although it helps them stumble along, it never becomes a part of them—it must be strapped on each day.

LLOYD JOHN OGILVIE

GOD THE ENEMY

The Reverend Doctor William Howell Emery knocked on our front door. I queried Arline. She had not called him to visit. He had not called her. I certainly didn't invite him to drop by, but I welcomed him heartily.

Bill Emery and I have become friends. I thoroughly enjoy the man. He has a rich sense of humor, a rare gift of preaching, from the pulpit, and keeps his distance. He has never tried to enter the fathomless recesses of my soul. We're able to work well together as elder and minister because we separate church and sentiment. My nomination to office came inasmuch as I'm able to confront groups and speak from strength and self-confidence. Concealed envies, resentments, and fears do not need equal time.

"Good morning, Bill. Making house calls now?"

"Yes, as a matter of fact. And I could stand a cup of coffee. How are you—and am I interrupting?"

"I'm fine, and you're not interrupting," I assured him.

We sat in the kitchen. Bill made himself at home with his

easy manner, becoming one of the family. He poured his own coffee, took milk from the refrigerator, and would have filled the sugar bowl if needed.

"How's the new company coming along?" he asked.

"After only six months of working at it, we're beginning to see some fruits," I vocalized. I wondered if he noticed my use of the word "fruits." It's so scriptural. I continued, "It takes time to get the image changed, Bill. For five years my clients have identified me with one studio. Now I'm asking film producers throughout the city to forget the old and to keep in mind the new hat I'm wearing. Most are not remembering."

"But surely some of those old customers you've told me about over the years are coming to you with work."

"No, they're not, Bill. I have no trouble getting the first or second lunch date, but actual jobs is another matter."

The memory of Don Andrews, and others, who repeatedly assured me they would always work with me, without regard to where I moved, hurts. Beyond question, I believed them and moved. Now everything we own is in jeopardy, and I find myself teamed up with a very slippery business partner.

Within three months of Dave Bartell joining the company, I could no longer live with Sid Steen. His demands upon my afternoons, my client lists, and support of Dave, bred chaos in my attitude toward the entire organization. Arline's incisive question months before had been answered as she knew it would be. I looked for work with other studios.

High paying offers did not come quickly this time. I spent many days planning and executing "accidental" meetings with principals of other companies. Drinking clients were recruited to speak favorably of me to other directors with whom they were working. I wanted these directors to seek my services, to ask their management questions pertaining to getting to me. It had always been successful. In the past, we would meet in an out-of-the-way bar, or restaurant, to discuss terms of employment. They would make the overture. It was a seller's market and I did not have to sell. Then the market changed on me. I had to buy my way into the Halstad Studio. But my name was on the door.

Bill Emery poured his third cup of coffee. "I'm sure it's going to turn out fine for you, Fred. I know the hours you spend in New York and the determination you have to succeed."

"Thanks, Bill. I need all the encouragement I can get. Now, suppose you tell me why you 'just dropped by,' " I said, "and don't tell me you were in the neighborhood."

"No, I wasn't just in the neighborhood. I thought I might find you at home on a Saturday morning. I need your help, Fred."

"You've got it, pastor, you know that," I said.

It's impossible for me to refuse church work when I'm asked by the senior pastor. My guilt for yesterday's hours in the city needs medication and Dr. Emery writes the prescriptions.

"I need someone with your ability to organize, to take over the responsibility of seeing to it that our monthly communion service runs smoothly."

"I serve communion whenever I'm asked," I boasted.

"Yes, I know, but that's not what I'm talking about. The system of calling elders to serve, the records of whom our past and present elders are, the proper assignment of them to the various areas of the sanctuary, is in such bad shape it will take all your talents to straighten the mess out."

"I hope I'll have the time for this, Bill." I looked for an excuse, an easy, logical way out. It didn't work.

"It shouldn't take more than a couple of hours. Once you get the files in order, you simply send out postcards one week before the communion service. I'll work with you on getting it started. How about it?"

"Do I have a choice?" I joked.

"Yes, but if you don't do it, you'll have to double your pledge."

"I'll do it. Owning thirty percent of the new company is costing us too much money. My partner and I are the last ones to get paid each week, and then not much."

That had been a condition of Tom Halstad's agreement to give me thirty percent of the stock. He and I take very little each week. My income dropped by over $10,000 a year. We expect to make it up as business improves. It hasn't happened.

I've learned my partner is not a film director in great demand. His work is good, but it's not exciting or unusual. He doesn't contribute significantly to the creative approach given to us, and he is confused about how much he is expected to add. He's also not in this country too often.

European by birth, Tom flies to the continent for any reason. He takes ten or more blank company checks with him, so I'm not only left alone for weeks, I'm forced to speculate the size of our bank balance on any given day. He returns when we have a production going, or when we run very low on cash. I continue in this relationship because of cowardice.

Where can I go? And for what reason this time? To admit I had made a monumental mistake will destroy my credibility in every advertising agency in the country. Accordingly, I have surrendered to circumstance. Each day feels like a day of bondage. I'm reluctant to initiate sales calls. It means I have too much free time for drinking and dreaming.

It's been over nine months since I promised myself success. I pledged decreased drinking, increased savings, and dramatic sales. Sid Steen got in my way. Forced to feed an ego and a deadly compulsion, I ran to a company position in which my word and action could not be challenged. My business card is a spectacle of exaggeration: "Fred Foster, President, Halstad-Foster Studios." Tom Halstad is Chairman of a nonexistent board of directors. He loves the title. I gave it to him so I could be president. Our small office overlooks Thirty-sixth Street. We rent stages when we work. We rent our people to do the work, and we even rent a very good European director/cameraman my partner knows from his past. We proudly refer to our staff as "free-lance." The size of our company is equal to the size of the current production. We're flexible. Previous clients and drinking cronies are not as pliable.

"Hi Don. This is Fred. I just received the oven cleaner scripts. Thanks a lot. We can use the business."

"I keep telling you we're trying to work with you, but I have not been able to until you got Conrad. His sample reel is terrific."

"It took some time, Don, but I really think we've got a winner in that young guy. Have you seen his latest feature release?" I asked with false calmness.

"Yes, and that was the touch I needed to convince Chicago that we should bid you on this one."

"You're quite a guy there, ole buddy. I can't tell you how much you've made my day. How about a drink?"

"Sure, but first tell me, is Conrad available to shoot this job in two weeks?"

"Yes. He just wrapped a London shoot, so he's yours."

"Okay. Do like old times. Put a small hold on him. I can't commit right now, but you know we'll work something out if Chicago leaves me alone."

"Great, Don. I'll meet you at P.J's in thirty minutes."

"Bring Conrad's oven reel with you when you come. The creative team in Chicago wants to see what he's done inside ovens."

I laughed wholeheartedly. "You haven't lost your sense of humor, Don."

"I'm not kidding, Fred. They asked me for commercials he's done for other oven cleaners. I've got them from the other two directors you're bidding against."

"Don, what's the matter with you guys? Conrad is one of the most creative and innovative cameramen in Europe, and you want him to prove he can light the inside of an oven?"

"It's not me. You tell that to Chicago. They're going to sit in a screening room and pick the film house from past experience in ovens."

"If I didn't know the crazy thinking in this business, I'd

swear you were putting me on," I slowly responded. "I'll call London in the morning and check with Conrad. He may have done an oven cleaner spot before. It's possible."

"I hope so," was all Don could say. Then he asked, "Do you still want that drink?"

I not only wanted that drink, I needed that drink! We each drank four martinis before dinner. Arline would not join us but assured me she did not mind driving home alone. She has a meeting again and I'm sorry I made the date with Don. Arline is spending too much time alone. It's not healthy. For me.

Six martinis, dinner, wine, cognac, and eighty-five dollars spent in Manhattan do not an oven cleaner sample reel make. That's not an old proverb. It's a fact of doing business with agency people who are so insecure that they look for their exact commercial on someone's reel before venturing into production. If the commercial turns out to be a flop, they will not be at fault because they used the experts who have done it before. We were not the experts chosen. Two days later Don told me we would not be bidding the job. We had lost it without even giving them a price. I took the hold off Conrad. He could remain in London and I could remain on Thirty-sixth Street. Alone.

I cannot understand what has happened to me. In search of new business, I've seen every one of my old clients. None have come through with an initial production assignment. I continue to come to this office every day of the week. The small black metal desk to which I report affords a view of a busy, noisy Thirty-sixth Street. I stand at the desk, phone to my ear, and observe life in New York City as portrayed on the dirty thoroughfare below. I picture the clients' desks, the office, and the excitement in which the phone I'm ringing sits. Secretaries answer, "He's around someplace, Fred. I'll have him call you if he can get the time." I call again, hoping they simply did not remember or they did not have the time to return my call.

"You just missed him."

"He hasn't returned."

"I gave him your message."

I no longer presume anyone has my message. How can they? I don't know the message myself these days. I've looked for it for years. It's now mostly found in bars when speaking with strangers. They know somehow the importance of my position in life. My card tells them and they believe. My success is not questioned. Pictures of my family document a happy and full family relationship. Buying drinks attests to my financial stability. So they hang around. The only subject which turns them away is religion. I only disclose my involvement with God to round out my person; to add credibility to everything else I've revealed. When my audience gets uncomfortable, I drop God. He's not too popular in cocktail lounges during the week. I pick him up again on Sunday. That's the day we're to talk to him, to let our needs be known. We've put the day aside for worship and some of us even contribute time and effort to the smooth running of the worship service. Tonight I'll be on the phone for hours getting men for this Sunday's communion service. I feel like a regular apostle.

"You've got the communion service well covered, Fred," Dr. Emery told me. We stopped to greet him after the service.

"I'm pleased with the way it went today," I said. "Everyone was here, even though it took some last minute phone calls to fill in the vacancies." I let him know the amount of work I did for his church.

Today proved to be a particularly difficult Sunday on which to assign elders to serve the bread and grape juice. I wondered how many I would get if I asked them to serve cocktails. The card system Bill suggested when I took the job was not the simple system he claimed, nor did it get results. The telephone, and laying on a little guilt, did.

It surprised me that men who have been members of this church for years, used shallow justification for not serving communion. Some were honest. They refused to do it by reason of not wanting to do it. No excuses. As each turned me down no matter how authentic his reason, I felt better about myself.

By comparison, I'm very much a Christian if willingness to serve is the yardstick. Whatever else is indefensible about me, my image of a loving, church-going head of his household is not at fault. I can feel clean about this, and I do. There's no particular presence of God or Christ around me. I don't think about that problem. I only go on enjoying the role of officer in a large parish which is over two hundred years old. Through the relationship, I look good in the neighborhood. A minister's name for a personal reference on a credit application does not hurt, either. His was helpful when we bought the summer home.

Bill Emery stopped Ken from bolting into the outdoors. "Are you ready for Nantucket, Ken?"

"I sure am, Dr. Emery. I can hardly wait." His voice smiled broadly.

We all laughed with excitement. I turned to my family and added, "Let's get going then. We've got a lot to do and we have a crowd coming over this afternoon." We were having the last "Sunday-after-church" cocktail party of the season.

Arline hesitated. She spoke to Bill. "Fred's finally going to take a week off, Bill. He's really taking some time to drive us up next week, and will actually stay with his family over the Fourth." While waving good-bye, she said, "We're all going to get to know him by name."

I understand the origin of her remark. The many late nights in New York, and the early escapes each morning, have made me a stranger in my own home. Our pastor friend interpreted her expression as concern for my well-being, put in jeopardy through the fact of hard work and long hours. His diagnosis was precise on one count only. I do put in long hours.

We said good-bye for July and August of this year. There would be no reason to say farewell next summer. I had,

unknowingly, set myself up to fail. While my family spends
the next two months on an island in the Atlantic, I will
spend the week days of this period striving to break loose
from inactivity, until each Friday afternoon when I'm
raised off the top of the Pan Am building and set free.

Cocktails and lunch in its Copter Club is my Friday exit
from the city during these hot months. From the spacious
cocktail lounge I feast on a spectacular view of upper Manhattan, and drink toast after toast to modern flight innova-
tions. At exactly two-fifteen I witness a helicopter's
approach. It lands on the floor above my martini, ready to
wisk me away from this concrete hell. I'm ready to leave in
a gulp.

On those few occasions when the weather is good in New
York and in New England, I leave from the heliport above,
connect with Northeast's three o'clock flight, and land at
Nantucket's colorful airport, one hour later. Thirty minutes
after landing, I sit on our porch, martini in hand, beholding
the beauty of the moors and sky. When we have bad weather, pilots are not the only people affected.

Flight delays promote summer friendships in familiar
airport bars. Many hours are played out, drinking and waiting. Clearance to drink is not required under these circumstances. We have little else to occupy our time as we listen
expectantly for our flight departure announcement. Most
stranded passengers leave me after they have had one or
two drinks. I don't know where they go. I only know I get to
meet many people as they take turns occupying the bar
stools on each side of mine. I stay put until all hope of
reaching Nantucket by air is gone. Then I search for ways to
go by land. Or sea. Or both.

I have journeyed to the weekend by driving a rental car
all night to Woods Hole, Massachusetts, arriving in time to
catch the six A.M. boat. The three-hour ferry crossing pro-
vides all the sleep for that night. Other Fridays have seen
me in Boston or Hyannis when "The Grey Lady at Sea" is
fogbound. Boston requires flight connections on a feeder

line to Nantucket. The Hyannis alternate requires fifteen or more stranded Nantucket fathers organizing into a force, now large enough to charter an all-weather boat. It also requires a very strong stomach in which to dump cold, greasy chicken and half a quart of straight scotch whiskey. The trick, of course, is to accomplish this gracious dining while standing on the fantail of a ship which seems bent on pounding its way across the entire Atlantic Ocean.

In jest I questioned being allowed to disembark in Europe without my passport. Arline invariably saves me by meeting the boat, heedless of the hour or weather. She looks so beautiful in the predawn rain, anxiously and lovingly searching. Each time she looks for sobriety. I rarely have it to give. I give, instead, other drunks. Strangers for distribution to their island families. She honors the promises I made during the tumultuous crossing. Through it all, Nantucket fathers have landed. Let the weekend begin!

Dear Pop,
  Even though you are a little chubby, I still love you. Sometimes you know me too well but that's because we are so much alike. Hope you have many more happy birthdays.

  Love,
  Ann

And then she drew a little smiling face.

Dear Dad,
  Thank you for the many things you have given me, especially Nantucket. I hope these next years are good ones, and I hope you have many more Happy Birthdays.

  Your son,
  Kenny

Their notes, in the Nantucket photo book they gave as their birthday gift to me, penetrated my heart and deeply frightened me. On this forty-eighth birthday, my family thanks me for this acre of land and windy moor. I cannot, dare not, face the possibility of its loss. A way of life is at stake. To keep it, my way of life must change. Please.

"I hope these next years are good ones, too, Kenny," I said. "I'm doing my best to make them good. That's why I haven't been up here much this year."

"That's okay, Pop," Ann offered. "We just miss having you around. It's more fun when we're all together."

"I know it is, Annie. And for me, too." I pushed an unfinished cocktail away. It sat denying everything I had said, so I rebuked John Barleycorn. He will not spoil a birthday afternoon with my family. Tonight, when Arline and I dine at our favorite local restaurant, I will be sober, to remember and to love my wife. Perhaps I can be filled with tonight all the nights of the coming week. Tomorrow I can have the strength to win.

"It always seems to be beautiful here on Monday mornings," Arline gently reported. She stood on the porch, looking over her beloved moors. "You'll have no trouble getting back."

"I know it. But once, just once, I'd like to be fogged in here for a few days. If I wasn't so concerned about Tom returning from England, and getting some business in the house, I'd stay."

"I realize that, Fred. But please be careful this week. Try to spend some time at home. I'm sure you've been invited to dinner in the neighborhood. You wouldn't have to eat alone."

"Okay, sweetheart. I'll get home—certainly tonight— and see that things are in good shape there. As for dinner, it will probably be an early one with Tom if he's back."

She took my hand as we walked to the car. "I don't want to spend all of the summer up here next year, Fred. Not if you're not going to be here more. I'm afraid of what's happening to us." It was not an ultimatum. It was one of the highest compliments she had ever given me.

She sat close to me as we drove to the airport. She's so

quiet. Worried about me—and us. I know I love this gal very much. I have never not loved her and I know I'm separating us. I silently vowed not to drink a single drink until I return next Friday. The closeness I feel for Arline this moment, I will maintain throughout the week by not drinking, and getting to our home early each evening. I will feel her presence and see her hand in each room. We'll talk for hours by phone each night, and my days will be filled with renewed efforts to succeed.

"Everything is going to be fine this week, Punkin." I held her close and looked directly into her trusting blue eyes. We parted at the gate, and I boarded the yellow DC-9 jet with the promise of righteousness on my lips and in my heart. I didn't know that the Source of strength I needed to secure this resolve sat with me as the speeding plane flew south. I made no attempt at contact, for I never looked his way.

Lunch with Tom Halstad is always interesting. He doesn't drink cocktails before eating, but knows how to finish a bottle of imported wine with dispatch. I drank no cocktails, but joined him in the wine. He also knows how to spend money we do not have.

"The film rights cost us only seven thousand, on a book which is the hit of England. Every producer in London wanted the rights, but because I know the assistant managing editor, I was able to move in." He sold hard. "It had to be done quickly, Fred, or not at all. Can we cover the check?"

"I don't know. We have only sixteen thousand still coming in from the Mercury job Conrad shot last month, and we owe the editor forty-five hundred, plus other suppliers more than thirty-five thousand."

"Have you sent them any checks?"

"No. I didn't know what checks you were writing in England."

"Good. The sixteen will cover England. When do you think it will be in?" he calmly queried.

"This week, for sure. But we need some of it for our own payroll, and fifteen hundred is due for August rent."

He reached across for more sweet butter and another roll. The table captain poured wine for each of us. "What do we have in new business coming? Anything for me to shoot?"

"Not right now. The summer has been slow for us. Many of my guys are on vacation, or shooting stuff we're not known for doing."

"I came back because I thought we'd have a lot of car spots in the works. What's with the boys in Detroit?"

"I haven't heard a word from them. You know most of the busy ones, Tom. Detroit never was my town, you also know that."

He looked up from cleaning his plate with a piece of bread. "I'll make some calls right after we leave here." There's no doubt he is the martyr come to save our company. I have let him down while he was busy in Europe trying to engineer the big deal for us.

My self-esteem needed help. "I hope you don't think I was sitting around while you were off in Europe for five weeks. There's just so many times I can call the same people with the same exciting story about my two directors being so busy elsewhere. They want to see new commercials we've shot, and I don't think we have anything decent to show." I keep forgetting that every time I point my finger at someone, there are three more on the same hand pointing back at me. He struck.

"How's the family doing in Nantucket? Been up there much?" It was a shot to make me feel guilty, and it did. Not because of weekends, but because of afternoons and evenings I now have trouble recalling.

"You know my summer schedule, Tom. I leave at noon on Friday and I get back by noon on Mondays. It's hardly worth the trip," I lied. "And no vacation with business so bad."

"Do you think we're going to make it—stay in business?"

He finished eating, wiped his mouth, cleaned his mustache, and sat back while I pondered his very pertinent question.

"I'm not sure. It doesn't look good right now, particularly with the cash flow in such negative shape. I sure hope your buy in England is going to pay off." I wanted him made aware of his responsibility to our cash position.

"That won't help us now, Fred. That's down the road about two years from now. We must have immediate business in the house or we'll go under. Have we paid our bill here? Can we sign for lunch?"

"Yes. I paid it last month. Your signature's good here."

He signed with a flurry. The captain's face told me the tip was big. We left. Silently.

Today was the first time in over a year that I have not had a martini with lunch. Not one! The wine did not do it for me. I feel sick. I'm emotionally incapable of dealing with my partner, with the business, or with the remainder of the day. The alcohol in the wine set off the compulsive switch again. I did not know the choice to drink had now been taken from me. I stopped Tom on the street.

"It's after two, and I'm due in Don Andrew's office. He may have some work for you. I almost forgot, what with you returning, and it being Monday," I concocted. Anything to get away from this man. Now!

"I'm certainly glad you remembered. How could you forget possible business?" Without waiting for an answer, he ordered, "Call me when you leave him."

I agreed to call, and headed for Madison Avenue. P.J.'s is only two blocks away. Some of the old crowd might still be there from lunch. It's not important they be there. I did not need an excuse for drinking today. The day offered the excuse. P.J.'s offered the answer.

The first drink is awesome. Its healing power is unprecedented. Every inch it travels to my stomach is memorable. Warmth and serenity invade. I take my first full breath of air, and relax my complete frame as I exhale. Peace embraces my entire being. Security sets in. I'm in a friendly surrounding which has shut out the street noise and hordes of charging people. There is no crowd. No pressure for answers. A cigarette fills my lungs with air I recognize. Smoke and gin adjust my mind. The world comes into focus. I'm in command again. No longer afraid. It's okay—tomorrow I'll stop for sure.

Tomorrow never came. Friday came. Four more Fridays came, and we closed the Nantucket house for the season. I switched my commute to the real Port Authority Bus Terminal, the one unaffected by weather or tourists. I thanked God for my family's return to New Jersey. I have reason for not drinking before commuting but I drink before commuting. I steal time and spend it in seedy westside saloons. It's here the problem drinkers are abundant. Those construction workers, drinking their shots and beer. That's heavy drinking. It's getting close to the bottom. Drinking in this part of town convinces me I am not an alcoholic. Walking from the bus stop to our lovely suburban home, the wide clean streets and the silence of the late hour, satisfy recurring suspicion. For the moment. The light in our bedroom put me on alert.

"Are you reading that thing again," I said sharply.

She put her Bible down and asked how I felt. She was genuinely interested in my day. She ignored my opening question. She smiled. It's midnight, and she smiles at me, welcomes me home. Usually when I'm in this condition, and at this hour, her back is to me. She covets sleep. Wants only that I leave her alone. Tonight she's asking questions, is willing to talk about the day. I want to forget the day. My entire world is falling apart, and now my wife wants to talk about the day. I'd rather she kicked and screamed. I had planned to go down to the kitchen and have some cognac before sleep. Her interest in my well-being, and her total inattention to my drinking, is destracting. I'm going to bed. I've had enough to drink.

I answered from inside the closet. "The day went pretty

good, hon." The wall held me upright as I removed my trousers. "We lost one job, but did get another one in. How was your day?"

She told me about her day in retailing on Fifth Avenue. I'm proud of the manner in which she has filled her life. I don't really enjoy her doing so much without me. It's disturbing and humiliating that she had to return to work. I feel I have driven her to it. Yet I'm proud of her. She's showing me a side I never saw before.

"When I called home earlier, Ann told me you were out with Betty Hancock again. Where in the world do you go with her?"

"Just to Alanon," was all she offered.

I had heard of this organization. It was, I recall, somehow connected to alcoholism. I became furious. "Are you going to these meetings because you think I have a drinking problem?"

She looked up from her reading, undisturbed by my outburst. "No. Not at all. I'm going because I have a problem."

That didn't make sense to me, but at least I thought I was not the reason. I climbed in bed as she turned out her reading light. In the total darkness of our room, her foot touched mine. Its tenderness shared her love and affection, amidst the discord. I silently pleaded with God to show himself—to help me stop my drinking. I don't know why I'm reaching for God; he's probably not even within hearing range. I didn't search long. Alcohol-induced unconsciousness launched me into tomorrow.

The shower feels good this morning. Again I have no evidence of a hangover, and no reason to acknowledge a problem with yesterday's alcohol. Six hours sleep always restores me physically and clears my mind. Clears it enough to fear the day.

Tom returns from Detroit today. This is his third trip there since his return from London, and he has not been successful. The Detroit agencies have not seen fit to award us new car announcement commercials and I'm almost pleased. My inability to sell the talents of this company is not unique. Tom's debacle in Detroit leaves me no choice but to quit. During his call yesterday, I told him of resigning, that I could no longer endure the pressures of a company going deeply into debt. Forfeiting weekly income has drained all our personal savings, and has forced me to put the Nantucket house up for sale. Tom asked me to delay my final decision until after we talked today. I have—but it's not changed.

"Not only is the company in bad shape, Tom, but I'm personally on the edge of bankruptcy. I cannot last without income. I must find work which will give me a weekly check."

"I understand your need for leaving, Fred, but I'm going to keep the company going. At least in name."

"Then I'll sign my stock over to you today. What are you going to do about the creditors?"

"They won't be a problem. I'll talk to them as they call. I expect to be gone for a month at least, so they'll have to wait until I return," he said calmly. "They'll be here when I get back—so don't worry about them."

I didn't have the time or the money to worry about the company creditors. Our own back taxes and many debts demanded all the delaying tactics I could create. The only asset remaining had to be called upon to satisfy our bills. Nantucket went. Arline and I painfully sold a dream. Surprisingly, I sold myself to another studio. One without cash problems and with six experienced film directors to sell. Within weeks I had reestablished myself with the Madison Avenue crowd. Arline and I were back to commuting together in our station wagon.

"This is wonderful, Fred. Your office is now only a half block from mine."

"I love it, sweetheart. We can walk from the parking lot to work, and meet easily at night." I lowered my cocktail glass. "This is a great place to meet. Why not make it the regular spot, then we'll each have a place to wait if the other is late."

A colorful Italian restaurant, unknown to either of us, only yards from our monthly parking, and in view of our buildings, became our neighborhood tavern. We soon knew the bartender, the owner, and the regular clientele. Everyone fell in love with Arline. We're the new couple on the block. We give them fresh topics of conversation, and exciting news from Hollywood. I have no interest in bus schedules or taxis. Our car rests close by, and Arline is with me. The only calls made home now are to inform Ken and Ann of our dinner plans. Often we remain, to dine with new friends and enjoy a few more drinks. Often we leave after Arline has had one drink, and the opportunity to observe my degree of sobriety.

She makes no comment regarding my condition. She enters, observes, then gently and firmly gives logical reasons for our immediate departure. I've become more aware of my inability to stop drinking once I've begun, so I continue to insist I will not drink tomorrow. Alcohol is not my problem, it's the circumstances under which I'm forced to work. Drinking has been thrust upon me, as fame has been thrust upon the Rockefellers. I was not born to this habit. I achieved it through constant and prolonged business drinking. And since business is good again, if Arline wants to go home early, I do not object. I finish the drink before me, and we leave. No argument.

"May I drive, Fred?" she pleaded.

"Why? I'm perfectly capable of driving. Come on, get in." There was no stopping me. I would drive.

Navigating the confines of the poorly lit, very narrow Lincoln Tunnel is more frightening for the passenger than the driver under sober operation. When I brushed off the side of the tunnel guard rail, Arline's loss of breath and gasped, "Oh, my God," sharpened my attention to the lane. For better focus, I cleverly closed my left eye. My right eye, the one Arline could see, remained open. I didn't feel drunk—only embarrassed. We both relaxed as we approached the wider highway and open fields of the Jersey meadows.

"Arline, I'm sorry about the swerve back there. I took my eyes off the road for a second, that's all it was."

Silence.

"Okay, you're angry. I'm sorry."

We drove in continued silence.

"You realize, Arline, the only reason I hang around town for you is because I don't think it's safe for you to be driving home alone so late. I worry about you on the street at night. You could get mugged walking to the car. That's all it takes."

"I'd rather take my chances with the muggers," she said softly.

We drove in more silence.

Arline stifled a laugh.

"What's so funny, Arline?"

"I can't help it. The more I think about you being worried about me and the muggers, the funnier it gets. You can calmly kill us in the tunnel, and then get upset because I may have to walk to the car. I really would be safer with the weirdos in town." She laughed freely.

I could see nothing comical about being mugged. It's far more dangerous than that little bump against the tunnel. That Alanon—or whatever it's called—is not helping me. Neither is her Bible reading. Or God. And I'm doing my share of work. Bill Emery has me serving on four church committees. He talked me into being chairman on one—the nominating committee. Now I'm choosing God's leaders. "Are you taking note, God?"

In quiet disbelief, Arline reached over and touched my arm. "Are you praying, Fred?"

I didn't realize I had spoken audibly. "No, but maybe I should. It's either that, or get out of this crazy business. I've got to do something." We pulled into our driveway.

"I know it, Fred. And I wish I could help. But you're the

only one who can help you. Except God." There was a hopelessness in her voice. A resigning. I hurt deeply. It is very difficult to live. There must be an answer. Somewhere. If I disentangle my life, I know the drinking will stop. Going into the city each day, and having daily client lunches forces me to drink. One does not take clients to lunch and abstain. Meeting Arline before driving home is another reason I drink—but I don't want to not meet. These are fun times together, but I must lessen the amount I drink before our rendezvous, or find a wider tunnel. I turned off the bedroom light. I will not forget this night.

"Do you mean to tell me you do not remember hitting the side of the Lincoln Tunnel last night?" she demanded.

"Arline, I don't even know what you're talking about. You drove home." I continued breakfast.

"I did not drive home. You drove home! I wanted to drive home, but you would not let me. Please get it into your head that you almost killed us last night." Tears came. She resembled a small, hurt child, who could not believe what was happening to her.

"You worry me, Arline. I really think you should not go to work today. And think about getting some help."

"Oh no, Fred. You're not going to do this to me. And I am getting help—exactly the help I need. Furthermore, I'm going to work today. Tonight I have to work until nine, so you can come home when you are ready. I won't get mugged, if that's still worrying you."

I couldn't understand why I would be concerned about her being mugged. Has she had people following her? The car incident puzzles me, also. I remember paying the garage man, but I do not recall driving home. Arline had to be the driver. But where did we eat dinner? I won't ask. Lately I'm being accused of making statements, performing acts, or offering promises which I absolutely do not believe originated from me. I pray we are not heading for separation—or divorce. On what grounds? Did I say I would pray?

There's a strange feeling going on inside me. I can't identify it, and it frightens me because it's so much bigger than any experience I've ever had. There's a presence I can't identify. I don't object to it. I simply can't touch it. I feel closer to this stirring during times of quiet and when I'm listening to Bill preach. He's been annoying my thinking lately. Upsetting my confidence. I'm pressed to jump off this speeding tiger, but I dread the fall more than the ride.

And where is God in all this mess? If he's here, and this be his way, then he's in the way.

We will know
as much of God
as we are willing
to put into practice—
and no more.
E. STANLEY JONES[8]

THE BORN-AGAIN DRUNK

The day had been a Saturday of my kind of recreation while Arline worked. I had mixed another gin and tonic—my fourth—before I left the house. I had napped and showered. The combination had produced a modicum of sobriety, which I maintained by not drinking martinis. So, by the time I arrived at the neighborhood cocktail party, I was able to think and listen while Dale Sheffield, a neighbor and golfing friend, engaged me in an intriguing challenge.

"I just came off a three-day retreat which I think you would like, Fred."

"I've never retreated in my life, Dale. And you're asking me to fall back? To give up?"

"OK, wise guy. You know what I'm talking about."

"Sure, I think I know what you're suggesting, but I honestly do not know exactly what goes on at a retreat, even though I've heard of them."

"First of all, forget everything you may have heard about retreats. This one consisted only of businessmen, just like you and me, and I can honestly tell you, Fred, it was the best weekend I have ever spent—and that includes our golfing trips."

"That's really saying something."

"Well, it's true, and I'd sure like to sponsor you for the next one."

"Sponsor? It sounds like a country club."

"It's no club, but it certainly is a special experience. It changed my life."

"I'm not sure I want my life changed," I whispered capriciously.

"I haven't changed my way of life as much as I've changed my way *to* life. I'm complete now."

"Why me, Dale?"

"Because you and Arline have shared some of your personal problems with us, and you know we've had some of our own. Even though I have lived in this town all my life, and have gone to school with most of the guys at this party, you're one I've felt close to, in the short time you've lived here."

"I thank you for that, Dale. I need all the allies I can get." I laughed defensively. I did not know how to react to his new brand of friendship. I did that which I do best—I retreated. "Can we talk about this during the week? Maybe have lunch over it. I'll buy."

"Fine. Whenever you want to make it," he confirmed.

"I'll call you," I said. "Excuse me for now though, as I must see someone before they leave."

He put his hand on my shoulder. "OK, I'll look for your call. In the meantime, have a good time."

"I always have a good time, Dale. That's one of the things I do best. It's the only way I can bear the rest of the garbage."

I turned away and heard him remark, "There's a better way."

I had no answer, for I have recognized a turning in this man. I can't identify the difference precisely, except the aura of peace I sensed about him. He's more free from strife than he's ever been—on or off the golf course. I'm very impressed with this shift in him, for Dale is solid, successful, a businessman who has followed all the proper steps to financial success and security. He's been with one company for twenty years, has no mortgage on his home, and can take early retirement with income for life. He has taken few chances. Why did he chance mentioning the retreat he's selling? And more—why is he taking a chance on me? I knew I would call him soon.

"This is not much of a restaurant, Fred, but it's quiet and we'll be able to talk. The food's not bad, either." He held the door open for me and said, "I'm happy you called and could make lunch so quickly."

We were given a small table against the back wall. The eating place was a glorified coffee shop. It had a bar. Dale ordered a highball, so I had my usual martini. After the first greedy swallow, I joked, "There it goes, Dale—I just felt my heart start. I'm alive again."

"I don't mean this as a play on words, Fred, but I need to talk to you about being just that—alive. I mean really alive—with your heart going all the time."

"I'll admit the subject holds some interest for me. That's why I called." I finished my drink and said, "Shoot." He shot.

He told me of the men who attended the three-day retreat, and of the change in himself. He spoke of peace—which I could not grasp. He offered security beyond material possessions—which I could not imagine. He spoke of having found the one answer to all of life's hazards—and with that promise he pushed a button in me. Although I did not want to be pressured into going on the retreat, I very much wanted that which I now observed in him. I could not shake the feeling I would fail to catch something big in the tide of events if I refused his invitation. I became serious about this critical juncture in my life. And this time I chose not to run.

Arline expressed delight when I told her I had signed to go on the retreat. Her endorsement added suspicion to the wisdom of my sudden irrational behavior, but Dale's announcement that I would not be the same when I returned awakened a spirit of adventure which outweighed thoughts of not attending. I became interested in the unknown, and the thought of a new perspective to living drew me. If I had known the punishment in store for me—from the long hours on my knees—I may have declined.

No amount of explanation could have prepared me for the weekend. The first thought which came into my mind was a question as to how I had allowed myself to get talked into the retreat to begin with. Here it was Saturday afternoon, and I had been abandoned for almost two days, with only a promise to be met again Sunday afternoon and ushered home. I hope I'm not forgotten, although I'm now not too eager to leave. We have been so engrossed with lectures, dialogue, and creative thinking, that these two days have been a challenge to my sense of showmanship. I've had opportunities to contribute intellectually and to speak out in questioning the application of religion to true life.

A furious summer storm beat down upon the Hudson River valley outside. Torrents of rain crashed against our windows. Eight men, their attention fixed, sat at each table in the imposing assembly room, which housed six spacious tables like the one at which we sat. Our table leader spoke. "Please, all of you, come with me," he whispered. Not one man at the other tables paid heed to our leaving. We were led to a small room, dimly lit by one candle. "Sit or kneel, whichever is the most natural and comfortable for you. Let's form a half-circle, facing the candle and the altar." He knelt at the end, next to me, and leaned forward. Smiling, he said, "For some of you, this may be the first time you have ever had the opportunity to speak with God, openly and in the company of other men. If you feel you don't want to say anything now, you don't have to. But if you do, just speak what's most on your heart, in your own way. Christ is here. And he's listening. You're very important to him, and he really wants to hear from you."

"I'll begin," he said softly. He immediately thanked Christ for each of us. He referred to him as Jesus, his first name. He spoke as though to a friend. My eyes moistened when he asked Christ to come into our lives. I seized control of my emotional response. His obvious friendship with God's Son surprised me. He actually knows the one to whom he's speaking. This simple New York City policeman, a cop in the traffic division, directs us effortlessly toward his Chief. He uses words of his street life, not the traditional "thee" and "thou" passages I've heard memorized for effect. This is the first time I believed a prayer has been heard. His closing, "So be it," rang with conviction. This guy expected his prayers to be answered. In the stillness which followed, they were. Silence can be explosive. It exploded in me. I forgot my knees.

I heard myself breathing from the depths of my abdomen. Air thundered in and out of my lungs. With closed eyes and bent head, I felt the back of my neck stretch to its forward extreme. My chin stabbed at my chest. I forced respiration, and entered the presence of the One whom I've known most frequently by names employed to profane. I heard my voice saying, "I don't know what I'm doing here, or why I came, but I think this is where I belong. If you are here, you know I'm confused, afraid of what's expected of me. You must know, also, that I honestly don't know how it is I believe." I paused, out of air again. I strained my eyes to control tears. I do not want sobs vocalized in the presence of these men. I restrained sentiment, and concluded, "I do want to believe, though, so show me how. Amen."

I did it! I prayed out loud. Now it's their turn. I relaxed, and listened to what they said. An awesome power took hold of our group. Hearts spoke. As though alone.

A seventy-five-year-old retired bookkeeper followed,

then a young dentist beginning practice in upstate New York; a computer programmer, newly married to his second wife; a stockbroker from Scarsdale, who's pleased it's raining today because he hasn't missed golf; and a magazine salesman from Manhattan's west side. Each speaks with God. The burning candle, our only source of light, has not flickered. The air is motionless. Weighted. Dialogue with God is going on. My competitive wish to be best vanishes. I only hear our side of the conversations, but someone is listening. Responding. And he is not the same someone who has been riding with me those Saturdays I seek escape and fellowship with wine and fish. Did I give them up when I said "yes" six weeks ago to the most extraordinary invitation I've ever received at the neighborhood cocktail party?

After a long quiet stay, we finally got off our knees. Each man had prayed. The experience of speaking in prayer awakened an inner need I had cowardly drowned with alcohol. An infantile craving for acceptance by everyone in my life came to the surface and released itself to a power outside of me. These men, with whom I've prayed, know I am troubled—that I'm not in control. Yet I feel stronger for sharing even one weakness.

This strange contradiction gained soundness from the balance of Saturday's program. The outer shell of my independence cracked. Life broke ground. The mortal Fred Foster became a willing receptor Sunday morning.

We assembled in the main chapel for prayer as we had done each morning. The weekend rain continued. Dark clouds refused to brighten the early July morning, but weather conditions are not important to me today. The arrival, one by one, of men who were strangers two days ago, and who are now very special human beings to me—is important. Our new community of comrades is gathering for praise and prayer before breakfast. The last hours together are upon us.

The now familiar, and welcomed silence embraced our world. We waited for opening prayers to begin. They were

late in starting today. A strange tone—as from the wind—
faintly penetrated our quiet time. The cadence of the un-
identified tone increased. It struck at my heart. I have
never perceived such a stirring harmony. Gradually I recognize it. The sound is human. People are humming.
Many voices are involved, and they're all tenors. No.
They're all women.

Into our chapel they come, humming the most captivating melody I've heard. I raised my head and turned toward
this fascinating manifestation of God's love. More than a
hundred women got up in darkness this wet morning to
show how much God loves me.

Standing before us, they carol a love song, an early morning love song from God. They sing of flowers which came
into bloom on the day I was born, of angels singing at my
birth, of a wish that they could get me a star from heaven.
They've come with a bouquet of carnations to sing their
song. The carnations remain, but they leave slowly, humming again until they, and their voices, which I imagined to
be wind, are gone.

Silence.

"I'm defeated, Father," I inaudibly prayed. "I don't know
what's happening to me, but I know I do not want to lose
what I've found." My folded hands catch tears. "Oh, Lord,
this is so difficult for me, but please come into my life. Take
it. Do with it as you will. I can no longer resist."

Complete exhaustion—physical, mental, and emotional
exhaustion rivet me to the pew. The wet world outside is
gone. It's Christ and me. I understand. I understand, at
last, that peace which is beyond understanding. How much
a miracle—to not know one second, and to know the next.
Only the Holy Spirit could bring this peace with which I
now look to today so hopefully. He did not deny his fulness
as the day unfolded in the final service. I knew I had received the one gift I could not have earned through any
amount of toil or sweat.

As it had been this morning, we convened in the beautiful, familiar chapel of this old seminary overlooking the mighty Hudson River. Hundreds of men before me carry the memory of this place with them, indelible in their mind's storehouse of life-altering decisions. I join them now, for the commitment made before breakfast this day has deepened. Each hour has brought new discoveries. I'm more intoxicated than on last night's communion wine, and higher than I have ever been in Manhattan.

These men, with whom I have just spent seventy-two hours, are brothers. Forever. One, in particular, has gained my love and deep respect. Scott Campbell is a self-confessed alcoholic. He will never be capable of moderate drinking. His alcoholism, his disease, will not allow moderation. Only complete abstinence. Through Christ he has a full life. There is no thought, need, or time for alcohol. I do not identify with his miraculous victory. Satan's powerful grip will not weaken until I, caught in this addictive vicious circle, want it weakened.

Pastor Paul, in his book, *Alcoholism*, claims God "certainly cannot make a sober man out of the guy who still wants to drink."[9] And I want to drink. And I want God. Can I have both? Scores of people have gathered in the chapel to share my new birth. They unknowingly also share my recruitment into spiritual battle. My Armageddon.

They fill the little chapel to capacity. Our reentry into society is supported by their demonstration of love. To help bridge the interval between three days of Christ-centeredness, and the reality of the world, they come. Our smiling guests have been to this retreat and faced the tests of living which followed. They know, first hand, the treasures here. They are eager to hear of the fortunes we have found.

Our songs have been sung, our prayers raised. We have praised God for the Body, his people. Now we are asked to speak of Christ within, to share the weekend with our guests. To refresh the memory of their own. I didn't know how much new Christians are able to feed the old. My turn to share came.

"I did not want to come, and now I don't want to go." I paused as they laughed. They know. "I wish the weekend could continue, and I know it cannot. Perhaps it's because I'm so concerned about how I'm going to handle Manhattan tomorrow. This morning, as the girls sang to us, I wept, as I'm now trying not to weep. I'm a salesman, so I know we each have our 'hot button,' that moment when the right words are said, and the sale is made. The 'sale' was made for me as you sang that lovely morning song. I asked Christ to come into my life then, to take it."

I stopped to breathe and to wipe my eyes. The heaviness of my lungs pressed against ribs. My chest cavity filled with emotion. I was drowning in new life. I scarcely held on. "Do you know what this means to a man of my ego? I've been told that to gain my life, I must first lose it. I'm not sure I know how to do that. You see, my favorite song has been, 'I'll Do It My Way.' And that's how my life has been—my way. But now I'm going to try it his way." I could speak no more. I sat.

They applauded me into the family. I saw Dale stand as he clapped his hands. He wanted me to know he has kept his promise to take me home. I felt relieved, and looked forward to discussing my excitement about Christ with him.

"It's almost five o'clock. Should we stop for a bite at this Howard Johnson up ahead?" Dale suggested.

"That's a great idea. I haven't had anything since lunch. Besides, I'd like to call Arline."

"You don't have to. I told her I'd have you home around seven."

I didn't call. I had a drink.

The hostess seated us at a table in the cocktail lounge. We simultaneously ordered drinks and dinner. I knew we would not delay eating, so I ordered a double manhattan cocktail. "Canadian Club, on the sweet side and straight up, with a dash of bitters." Dale had his usual one weak highball.

"Well, Fred, you look as though you've been hit hard.

How'd you like it? From the sound of your testimony, you found something."

"I think I did. And, Dale, I can never thank you enough for talking me into coming up here. This has been the most fulfilling and the most fun weekend of my entire life. I have never laughed so much, nor cried so much, ever."

"Don't thank me. God had a hand in this. He only used me to get to you."

"He sure did get to me. And to think eternal life is a gift. That's what blows my mind. There's nothing I could do, or have done, which has earned me this prize. I cannot believe, as yet, that Christ picked me. Why me? Why not that guy sitting over there?"

"I can't answer that, Fred. I can only tell you it's real."

"I've never believed Christ to be alive for our time. I believe that now, Dale. Will this feeling last? Has it for you?"

"I've had to work at it every day. I'm reading the New Testament, and I'm praying every morning. Did you get a copy of *Good News for Modern Man?*"

"Yes, and I'm going to start it tonight if it's not too late. I don't want to lose this feeling, Dale. I fear that more than anything right now."

"I know you learned the importance of continuing in fellowship with other Christians as a means to growing in faith. We have a prayer group going in our office. You're welcome to join us, Fred."

"Do you mean to tell me prayer groups meet in Manhattan? In office buildings in Fun City?"

"That's what I'm saying. Our group is so large we meet in the board room. Once a month. We share God's working in our lives."

"I don't believe what I'm hearing."

"It's true," he said. "Scott Campbell is leading the next one. He's going to report on this very weekend of yours."

"You mean Scott the. . . ."

"Yes," he interrupted, "Scott the alcoholic."

Scott Campbell taught during the weekend. He gave a powerful and moving account of being a recovering alcoholic. It embarrassed me when he spoke of how much he drank, for he displayed no guilt or remorse for his degrading life experiences while drinking. His assertive stance regarding his relationship with Jesus Christ added to his uniqueness in my mind. I never imagined alcoholics to look as poised and self-confident as Scott. I found it difficult to believe he ever drank, and I had trouble believing his personal relationship and devotion to Christ. He looks like a bank president—not a drunk, or a Jesus freak. Admitting to weaknesses and the need for strength from others—he was certainly unlike the kind of Christians I know.

Dale then told me of the work Scott does with alcoholics. "He is really one terrific guy, Fred. He's been sober for over ten years now. Been in AA all that time."

"Yes, I know. He mentioned that during his talk Saturday."

"I know he didn't tell you of the number of men he has literally returned from the living dead, because his creed for his own living is, 'Do something nice for someone every day, and don't get caught doing it.' "

"Does he go out and look for drunks?"

"No, not that. But he doesn't hide the fact that he is an alcoholic, and that it's not a sin. I've heard him talk of his 'disease'—that it's not a social stigma."

I had heard that Saturday. He also told us how deeply he fell during the drinking years. He lost jobs, home, and family. He talked about hitting the bottom—spiritually, mentally, and physically. Compared to him, I'm certainly not an alcoholic. Fear of being addicted to liquor lessened after hearing Scott. I would not deny I drink heavily, but evidently I'm not going to ruin my life over a few drinks. Scott will not have to reach out to help me, that's for sure. Besides, I've done all the reaching necessary. I reached for Christ and he took my hand. It was the sober hand, though. Inside of me, the drunk which is me, lies in wait for the first drink, which releases a born-again drunk, and I don't even know it. Arline knew it when I entered the bedroom. I could tell by her kiss.

"You look as though something has happened to you, Fred. How was it?"

"It was really great, hon. Quite an experience, to say the least."

"Are you going to read that?" she asked, pointing to the New Testament I carried. Her voice and expression telegraphed her recall of the countless times I admonished her reading God's Word.

"I know, honey, after all the times I badgered you, but I'm going to take a fling at it. They told me that if I didn't read, and continue to find out more about Christ, I would soon lose contact with him."

"Something has happened to you."

"Well, I broke down today. I asked Christ to come into my life, to take it. And I feel better. I'm relieved of a burden I didn't even know I carried and I can't identify."

"You haven't stopped drinking, though."

I should have had vodka before dinner. Canadian Club whiskey leaves telltale odors. "Drinking is not my problem. It never was as far as I'm concerned." Arline did not respond. "I really don't know what is going to happen now," I continued. "All I know is that I don't feel so much in charge of things as I did a few days ago, and that I'm going to try to find out more about Christ and his power."

"I think that's really terrific, Fred, and I'm very happy for you. You deserve to be happy, and I pray this is the beginning for you."

"Thank you, sweetheart. That means a great deal to me." I held her close. Her beautiful face, so innocent and searching, studied my every move—then moved away when I suggested we have a drink before going to bed. We descended to the kitchen.

The snifter of cognac, cupped in the palms of my hands for warming, did not excite me tonight. I enjoyed the feeling of it going down, but I derived no pleasure from its taste. Arline drank tea, and described an uneventful weekend at home. My return is upsetting. I'm a stranger in long-established surroundings. My own home, with my own wife and customary drink before retiring, is perplexing. I slid the cognac away and said, "I've had enough of this for now. I'm really tired. Let's call it a night. Okay?" She agreed.

I left the unfinished cognac. It does not belong in tonight's feast. The wine used in last night's communion service belonged. It represented the blood of Jesus, shed for me. When I drank it, the compulsive switch turned on for I had not chosen the harmless grape juice which was available. I wanted the wine the disciples drank, and used one of the best excuses for drinking ever discovered.

The Saturday night fellowship which followed communion was meant to be a love feast, during which a glass of wine is shared between new brothers. I overdid it, just as I overplay living. I shared many glasses of wine with many brothers. Alcohol had been made available. I found it. Christ had also been made available, but I ignored him and got drunk at his supper, only to find he wanted me regardless of my condition.

In years to come, I would learn that the disease of alcoholism caused my drunkenness, whereas for most people, being drunk is a temporary condition which passes when they become sober. I would also learn that alcoholism is the one disease from which recovery is possible only after its victim has grown spiritually. Otherwise, early death is assured.

"Will you pray with me, honey?" I asked. She put her Bible aside and looked up from her reading position in bed. Her expression could not have been for me. It communicated uncertainty, as if I were a stranger standing beside her.

"Pray with you? Now?"

"We've never really done it before. I would like to thank

the Lord for the day and ask him to bless our home and family for the night. Would you kneel beside the bed with me?"

As though obeying an intruder, she moved to appease my bizarre request. "You actually want to kneel?" she asked. "Now? Together?" And then, resigned to cooperating, said, "That really must have been some weekend!"

"I can't help it, Arline. I have to close the day somehow and I don't know of any other way than to pray about it." She got on her knees beside me. Not with me in approval, but with me physically. It was enough.

"Lord," I prayed, "I still don't know what I'm doing. I only know I want to talk with you. So now I thank you for these past three days and for coming into my life. I thank you for Arline being here when I returned, for Ann and Ken, and our home. Bless each of us now. Protect this home during the night, and walk with each of us tomorrow. I ask this in Christ's name. Amen."

We rose silently. "It wasn't much of a prayer, Arline, I know. But it's the best I can do right now. I'm still new at this." Without comment, Arline returned to reading. I opened the New Testament. At the beginning. For the first time.

I read about Jesus' ancestors and the facts concerning his birth. And then I slept the best sleep I had in years. The spirit used this night did not come in a bottle. He had come on a cross to be with me, even as I shut him out of cocktail lounges during the months ahead. A more determined Satan drinks with me as he has for years. Bars belong to him and to drinking clients who do not know Christ, and who have not heard of him through me.

"What's happened to my drinking buddy?" asked Don Andrews. "You're acting as though you're a thousand miles from here, Fred."

"I'm here, and nothing has happened, really. But do you remember when I told you about that weekend I went on two months ago?"

"What's that got to do with us having lunch? You need another martini."

He didn't even ask me to tell about my experience. Thwarted, I took his advice, ordered the martini, and did not try to tell him about God. In the two months since the retreat, I have not told anyone outside of church the gift which he wants to give freely. The impact of asking Christ to come into my life has diminished. Cocktail lounges and drinking separate me from Christ, yet, being with people who do not want to speak of Christ or religion is uncomfortable. They're not as much fun as they were previously. Neither am I.

Fear of rejection, of ridicule and loss of business, prevent me from expressing Christ. Drinking with them is our only common ground. These people, these restaurants, and my profession are life as I know it. I have fought and drunk my way back into favor after the chaotic period of partnership with Tom Halstad. I don't want to lose income again. I want to fit Christ into television commercials. My way.

"If we won't walk after God's heart, he lets us walk after our own heart's desires. If we won't hearken to his voice, he lets us walk according to our own voice, and what desperate consequences accrue. The moment we feel that we can 'do it,' God stops doing. If we're going to be our own defense, God will get out of the way."[10]

Early morning study and prayer hours introduce me to new words, powerful thoughts, and no escape. It's his one-way street, which I desperately crave during the silent, peaceful morning of each day. These hours are keeping me whole, for alcohol has taken its toll. Five martinis are required at lunch. Afternoon drinking is now constant, and alone. I'm being torn apart by Jesus. Or Satan. Faith is a blessing in the morning and a burden in the afternoon. Completely unable to handle alcohol, I turn to study feverishly. Spirit-filled authors give me strength and resolve. Bars filled with spirits give me guilt and despair.

Lunch comes earlier each day. It's a descending spiral of self-destruction not recognized because I don't drink before lunch. Drunks drink before lunch—and before breakfast. I read and pray before breakfast. My needs are shared with God, and God reveals to me his commands for living—not for dying as drunks die.

My copy of the Bible contains 735 pages of Old Testament writings. To read the entire ancient chronicle in one year requires I read only two pages each morning. I can handle this, only I don't understand much of what I'm reading. The Bible is too big for me right now so I'm just giving myself an introductory exposure to it. I'm not concerned with where all the study is taking me, for I'm unable to think too far beyond today. The strength I receive in prayer after reading Scripture, gets me going on a positive note. Christ continues to feed me, to dress my mind with his power. I know without question, that he is present through his Spirit. I feel him in our living room, and then lose him in the dining rooms of New York City when drinking.

I have yet to talk to Christ about drinking. There is for me no correlation between being drunk and being born again. Drinking is normal to my way of life. Getting drunk simply comes from too much alcohol and the pressures of that way of life. The monthly fellowship meeting in the board room of Dale Sheffield's company becomes my only safe harbor in Manhattan. Here I can use his name in praise, and find love not dependent upon performance.

During the second meeting I attended, Scott Campbell deliberately sat next to me and asked, "How are you doing, Fred? Everything all right?"

"Quite well, Scott. Thank you for asking."

"If I can ever be of any help to you, in any way, just give me a call," he said as he handed me his business card.

"Okay. But say—while you're here, would you answer a question for me?"

"Certainly, if I can." He moved closer.

"These prayer meetings once a month are really great. I can't tell you how much your position on life, with regard to Christ I mean, affects my thinking. But I have a great deal of trouble telling clients and fellow workers about Jesus. Do you bring up his name during the day when you're making calls?"

"I seldom initiate the conversation, Fred. But when the subject of religion, or my way of life is brought up by the other person, I tell them about my relationship to Christ. I never talk religion. I talk about the results of a religious experience."

"That's a big help, Scott. You see, I feel so guilty for not telling clients, or others, about him when I think I should."

Scott leaned forward, put his steady hand upon my shoulder and looked into my eyes. "Fred, you don't have to feel guilty about anything. You're a very special person to Jesus Christ and, in fact, to me."

The praise embarrassed me. "Thank you," I choked.

"It's true. And I see in you a person who is going to be a serious witness to Christ in your life. He's making changes as we speak, and for some of us, change takes time."

"It seems to be for me, Scott. It's been over two months since my weekend, and I haven't done too much to glorify his name. I'm trying to protect my own and I know I shouldn't care about that."

"Christ never said you shouldn't care about protecting your own life. He did say you must give it up to find true life. Being concerned about your life, and protecting yourself and family, is natural. We're still human beings, all of us."

"I guess that's where my battle is. I want to be me and I want him to be in me. But even with the battle, Scott, I know the joy we talked about during those three days. Not only am I not worried about where he's leading, I'm happier than I have ever been in my whole life."

Scott stood in preparation for leaving. "Praise the Lord for that. Now remember what I said about being ready to help. Just call me whenever you have the urge. I have to catch a train now, but I'll be praying for you every morning from now on."

"I'm negotiating with a California film company, so I can

use your prayers. God bless you, and have a safe trip home."

"You're not planning a move to the west coast, are you?"

"No. We'll never leave New York, but I'll probably leave my present position to work for this new company. They want to get going in New York, and think I can do it for them."

"Whatever you do, God is with you in it," he said in parting.

I could not believe God would want to be with me in this present conglomeration of suspense.

My career is in serious jeopardy because I lose time from work due to drinking. I'm aware of this for the first time. Arline and I are not on the best of terms. Drinking is making our home life unhappy. She goes from one success to another in her fashion world, while I call only upon old clients who still like to drink at lunch. Remorse after drinking is a constant companion. Guilt overwhelms. Renewed drinking erases guilt while I'm intoxicated, but each time I use the bottle, it is less effective in providing the escape.

To combat these diminishing returns, I spend more and more time in the west side bars before going home to late dinners, which I bless with slurred words to an uneasy family. Drinking and praying are not compatible. Drinking and selling are compatible and never more so than with a long forgotten Air Force associate who is looking for a film studio to produce his commercials.

"How did you know where to find me, Gordon?" I asked.

"I read about you in *Ad Age*. It was the announcement of you changing jobs. Normally I don't read those personnel change items, but there are times, even in Boston, when there is little else to do on a rainy afternoon."

"I don't believe it. Not in Boston."

"Yes, and even in a small agency like ours. We're not like some of you big boys down here who pack up and head for the suburbs when the weather gets bad."

"Well, it was the surprise of the year when you called me

with some commercials to do. I didn't even know you were in the same business, much less out of the Air Force."

"It's a stroke of luck for me, Fred. I don't know the first thing about producing commercials, and all of a sudden we get a candy account that wants to go national. I didn't want to open this job up for bidding with studios I've never heard of. I was also afraid of getting ripped off by the sharp film crowd in the big city. Then I remembered your name, because I was going to write to you anyhow. There was just no one else for me to go to. No one I could trust. So I called you."

"Well, I'll sure take you through it step by step, so the next time you can know as much as we do. But first tell me, do your people know they're talking about a ton of money for twelve days of shooting?"

"Sure. We're thinking it will take somewhere around two hundred thousand by the time we're through. The air time they're buying will run over five million, so we're after the brass ring on this ride."

I had done it again. Unexpectantly I had brought in one of the largest sales of my career, without effort or competition. It secured my position with the company. They could not fire me as long as Gordon's job remained unfinished, and Gordon was in no hurry to finish. He loved drinking and Christmas in New York. I gave him both. Abundantly.

Gordon became the hit of every luncheon huddle to which I took him. His huge job renewed my prominence along Madison Avenue. Word of my coup reached California, and California came calling.

A Hollywood-based film company, with offices established in New York, asked me to head their Manhattan division. I took the attitude they were football scouts, seeking the number-one draft choice. If they were to get me, they would have to give me a three-year contract, a good salary, five percent of gross sales and a cash bonus for signing. They met all terms. We agreed to begin January second—the first day of work in the new year.

Three weeks before Christmas I had a very promising new position and only one important client to entertain. Drinking began at eleven-thirty each morning, and occupied the entire working day. Although I had resigned to accept the California offer, Gordon's job needed my attention. I promised management I would not leave until Gordon felt satisfied. He proved to be a difficult man to please except when drinking. Then he wanted to please everyone else. Particularly during the Christmas season. When we were both drunk.

"Let's go buy a present for my wife, Fred."

"Okay."

"Let's go where your wife works and get something there. She could help me find a nice present."

"That's fine with me. Arline sure knows what women need for Christmas," I mumbled. "She's in charge of the entire men's specialty shop for Christmas. We can even get a drink there. They have a bar for us businessmen."

As we entered Arline's world, I spotted her immediately. She came running when Gordon fell into a pile of gigantic cushions. He took an umbrella stand with him, but didn't hurt himself or damage the cushions.

"Please leave, Fred. Please," she pleaded. "And take him with you before I'm forced to call security."

"Take it easy, Arline. We only want to get something for his wife. He'll be okay."

"We will not serve drunks. It's against store rules. And if you don't leave immediately you will not see me at home. Ever."

The pain and embarrassment in her eyes told me the depth to which I had fallen and to which I had taken her in the presence of her staff and customers. I helped Gordon to his feet. We departed as quickly as we had come in.

"I've had it for today, Gordon. I can't drink another drop. You'll have to excuse me for the rest of your trip. I'm going home, and I think you should do the same because the commercials are finished and we both know it. Have a Merry Christmas."

He looked at me from eyes almost rolling in their sockets. "Yeah, you're right. It's time to go home. Merry Christmas to you and thanks for everything. See ya around." He left. I didn't enjoy being alone. Not with only me to talk to. I hailed a cab. The Port Authority Bus Terminal witnessed another holiday drunk heading home. I needed an office party on which to place the blame. I've never felt guilty about drinking while drinking. It comes later. Tonight I'm guilty of embarrassing Arline so severely that I am unable to forgive myself. I cannot find a satisfactory rationale. It's Christmas. I hurt deeply because I have just hurt Arline so deeply. Where is Christ this year?

I searched my pockets for Scott Campbell's card and a dime.

From the privacy of her office, Arline phoned Dale Sheffield.

Dale Sheffield phoned Scott Campbell.

I had a lunch date. A life-altering lunch date arranged in heaven.

When I spoke to Scott about lunch, he asked if it was all right that Dale join us. I consented. Dale must know my need. He really started me on this struggle with alcohol and Scripture. We met the next day. Everyone was unusually free of business dates.

"Will it bother you, Scott, if I order a drink?" I asked.

"Not at all. Help yourself." Unabashed, he ordered milk.

"Before the drinks get here, I've got to say something, Scott. Do you mind if I get right to what's troubling me?"

"That's a good idea. What's the problem?"

"I think I need your help. I've been drinking too much lately. It's affecting everything and everybody in my life. And yesterday was the worst. I think I would like to check Alcoholics Anonymous out with you. If you'll take me."

"I'll be glad to take you, Fred. Let me first say that what you have just done, admitting to a drinking problem, is the single most important step you will ever take in your life. Next to your becoming saved through Christ, of course."

Dale put his hand upon my sleeve. He neither condemned nor agreed. He supported me, and my courage.

"I think I know you," Scott continued. "I know you better than you think. I believe you're the kind of guy who needs a significant date as his anniversary day in AA, so I'm not going to ask you to stop drinking right now."

"Not today?" I asked.

"No. It's two weeks before Christmas. I know you have parties planned, and that you're having people over for New Year's Eve. So continue drinking until then."

"Until when?"

"New Year's Eve. That's when I want you to stop. When the ball in Times Square reaches bottom. You watch that on television, don't you?"

I assured him we always watched the New Year in on television.

"Good. Then you'll begin next year dry. At the stroke of twelve. Remember that."

"I'll give it a try, Scott. But New Year's Eve is the one night of the year when I can get drunk and look normal. And you want me to stop when it's really just starting?"

"I know that. I've been there many times."

"I guess you have. I forgot you know what it's like."

"If you want what I have, freedom from drink, then you must do as I ask. Okay?"

"Okay. You're on."

"In the meanwhile, don't drink the town dry." He laughed, and added, "Even you can't do that."

"Maybe not, Scott. But I sure had them working nights."

"So did I. Don't worry about the guys who make it. They'll get along fine without you and me."

We finished lunch without further drinking. I felt relieved. That strange paradox of sharing weakness and finding strength worked again. Would it work for New Year's Eve?

Our guests quieted their revelry to fix their attention upon the televised extinction of another year. The electric ball on the Times Square tower embarked upon its annual sixty-second voyage into next year.

As the ball decended, I looked forlornly at the crystal stem glass in my hand. I raised it to my lips, and emptied it of the superb French wine it held. I laid it to rest on a nearby coffee table. The electric ball in Times Square came to its final destination in recording history. I turned to embrace Arline.

"Happy New Year, darling."

"Happy New Year, Fred. I pray this will be a special year for you. And with the Lord's help, I know you'll succeed in this new life, and with the new company."

"Thank you, Punkin. The Lord will have to do it. I don't know if I can stop, but at least I've had my last drink for this night. That's all Scott asked me to do—stop at midnight—for the night."

"You'll make it, Fred. I know you will." She kissed me and I knew we still had a chance. It's my choice.

"Help me with tomorrow, Lord," I silently prayed. "You know how much I like to drink during the Rose Bowl game."

I needed a few miracles to win this one.

And I don't even know what a miracle looks like.

He
who limps
is still
walking.
SWISS
PROVERB

8

GOD THE FRIEND

Wednesday, January 2. The first work day of the new year. The center of the humidity-veiled window I wiped clean with my leather gloved hand, is the only aperture through which I can survey the dark grey outside. In the midst of freezing rain, mixed with snow, New Jersey's marshlands pass in view.

I long to be anywhere other than on this congested, overheated bus going to Manhattan. It's taking me into the environment I once used for escape. Today I'm afraid. I believe Christ is with me, yet I feel alone in the encounter I must face. Alone because I'm new to sobriety and to the hours ahead of not drinking. A painful feeling of impending danger overtakes me. I'm reminded of times past when I promised myself I would not drink a martini at lunch. I would compromise with wine because of too much drinking the night before. Even that concession to alcohol could not be kept. Is today any different?

Within me, the born-again drunk, now sober, does seek

the will of God. Yet I go, using my power of determination
to give birth to a new film company spawned in the minds
of men just now awakening to their Wednesday morning in
Southern California. They do not know this is only the
second consecutive sober day I've lived in over three years.
They do not know of my resolve to conduct their New York
company's business as nearly balanced as I can to ethics
which are Christian. They do not know the failure I fear
from the selfsame clients they need for success. These men
with whom I can no longer drink, or manipulate. My new
employer believes the first thrust will be in search of new
production. Yesterday Scott Campbell told me to first seek
sobriety.

"When you think of taking that first drink, Fred, don't
just think of the drink itself," he advised. "Think the drink
through—to its ultimate conclusion and what will happen
to you because you drank."

To help me not drink this first day in New York, Scott
invited me to lunch. He wants to welcome me into his
"club." I now know the club to which he referred. It's an
immediate bond between two recovering alcoholics. He
understands the fight I've entered. I appreciate the battle
he has waged for ten years.

"Okay, Scott," I yielded. "I'll do whatever you say. Lunch
is fine with me."

A drowning man does not first test the seaworthiness of
the rescue craft before clutching the hand that lifts him
aboard. In my determination to stay afloat, I seized on
Scott's phone call and request for lunch, and met a
phenomenon. The first of many miracles. I did not drink a
martini, a manhattan, or so much as a single glass of wine
during thirteen hours of college football. Scott's call had
linked me to a recognizable victory. To a man, much like
myself, who had been a practicing alcoholic. We share a
common failure. Can we now share a common triumph?
My family has no feeling either way.

Years of disappointments have bred skeptics. Arline can only watch—and hope. Ken and Ann doubt. Length of sobriety, and my ability to abstain from drink, is silently predominant in every thought and function of the holiday. Supportive at home, they know they must leave me to New York. Manhattan is my supreme battleground. It must be won. On bar stools. During client lunches. Repeatedly. Alcohol will always be visible to me. I must learn to live with it in its environment without it controlling my days.

The city is one huge cocktail lounge to me. Bars are everywhere I turn. The drunkard in me trembles during the taxi trek across town to Second Avenue, site of the two-hundred-year-old brownstone which is my new base of operations. One day of sobriety is a very fragile gift with which to begin building. I cannot imagine going through lunch without drinking. How will I use the time? What will I talk about for two sober hours? Scott answered these questions when we met for what I thought would be a quick lunch.

"We're going to an AA meeting. It begins precisely at 12:30, and will end just as promptly at 1:30. So, if you have a two o'clock appointment, you can count on making it." He shook my outstretched hand throughout his announcement.

One hour of worry vanished.

"If you have no appointment today, we'll go and have lunch after the meeting."

Two hours of worry vanished.

He led me into a side door of St. Thomas Episcopal Church. Inside the tiny elevator he asked, "How are you feeling?"

"Pretty good," I smiled. "I'm a little frightened because it's a strange New York in which I find myself today." The elevator doors opened to a throng of noisy, laughing people.

"Welcome to your first AA meeting, Fred." He gave me a

firm pat on my back. "You'll meet lots of nice people here.
They all want to help, and some of them are even in your
business."

Over two hundred sober alcoholics smiled at me, at
Scott, and at themselves. They had lived through another
round of holiday parties and excuses for drinking. I knew
Christ led me here. I see his hand everywhere, and no
more so than in the face of an agency film producer I had
not seen for years. He recognized me.

"Fred Foster," he laughed. "I won't ask what you're
doing here. I'm only glad that you are."

"Well, I'll ask what you're doing here. I never thought
you drank too much. You didn't when we had lunch."

"Lunch was only the starter, Fred. You may recall that I
usually left before eating. I stayed for the cocktail hour
only. Food got in the way of the glow I needed, and it took
time away from drinking just to eat it. Someday I'll tell you
all about it. For now, it's good to see you've made it."

"I hardly feel as though I've made it. This is my first
meeting."

"That's great. Keep coming back, Fred. And look, I'm
still working for the same shop, so if you want to have
lunch, call me. We'll dutch it. Now I'll have lunch with you
again. I had to stop seeing guys like you when I stopped the
booze."

That came as a relief. For two years I thought he stopped
because he didn't like the directors I represented, or me. I
promised to call.

This first AA meeting, in a church on Fifth Avenue which
I have passed hundreds of times, shatters my preconceived
ideas of alcoholics. Well-groomed, bright-eyed, intelligent
people fill the room. Laughter and acceptance rule. I expected lunch with Scott to be helpful, but I could not have
imagined the support I would receive from so many whom
I did not know before today. Their presence here tells me I
am not isolated. Or unique.

I don't remember much of the meeting. We were asked

to share if we felt the need, and to identify our disease before speaking. During a moment of waiting for someone to speak, I stood. "My name is Fred, and I'm an alcoholic. This is my first meeting, so I haven't much to say except I think I'm in the right place." I actually heard my own voice declaring me to be an alcoholic. The confession startled me. Their applause welcomed me.

As I sat, Scott leaned over and whispered, "Keep coming back. It gets better all the time."

I told him I would come back, then silently questioned my rash demonstration and impetuous disclosure. Am I really an alcoholic? Can't I stop for awhile and then go back to it sensibly? How can I be certain I'm never going to be able to drink again? Scott answered these questions for me. He had not heard. But he knew. Christ had come to the meeting. Prayers were being answered, and coincidences were going far beyond chance.

"Before we leave, Fred, pick up some of the reading material here. It's good stuff. Particularly this one." He handed me a yellow card entitled, "Are You an Alcoholic?" It's used by Johns Hopkins University Hospital in Baltimore. The title was enough to dare me. I sat and took the test before we went to lunch. My answers to the test questions could not be ignored:

1. Do you lose time from work due to drinking?   YES
2. Is drinking making your home life unhappy?   YES
3. Do you drink because you are shy with other people?   NO
4. Is drinking affecting your reputation?   YES
5. Have you ever felt remorse after drinking?   YES
6. Have you gotten into financial difficulties as a result of drinking?   YES
7. Do you turn to lower companions and an inferior environment when drinking?   YES
8. Does your drinking make you careless of your family's welfare?   YES

9.	Has your ambition decreased since drinking?	YES
10.	Do you crave a drink at a definite time daily?	YES
11.	Do you want to drink the next morning?	NO
12.	Does drinking cause you to have difficulty in sleeping?	YES
13.	Has your efficiency decreased since drinking?	YES
14.	Is drinking jeopardizing your job or business?	YES
15.	Do you drink to escape from worries or trouble?	YES
16.	Do you drink alone?	YES
17.	Have you ever had a complete loss of memory as a result of drinking?	YES
18.	Has your physician ever treated you for drinking?	NO
19.	Do you drink to build up your self-confidence?	YES
20.	Have you ever been to a hospital or institution on account of drinking?	NO

I answered *yes* to sixteen of the twenty challenges used by Johns Hopkins. Their yellow card told me how to score my test results:

"If you have answered *yes* to any one of the questions, there is a definite warning that *you may be an alcoholic.*

"If you have answered *yes* to any two, the chances are that you *are an alcoholic.*

"If you have answered *yes* to three or more, *you are definitely an alcoholic.*"

I could not deny the miracle of my New Year's Eve decision, for in like manner, Webster tells us a miracle is thought to be due to supernatural causes, especially to an act of God. It's an act of God for me to be at this meeting, not drinking during this hour of the day. And, unless this test is too severe, I'm very much an alcoholic. During lunch I asked Scott about the test.

"Yes, it's a tough one, Fred. But only to those of us who have a drinking problem. To anyone who does not drink, or who drinks moderately, the test is simple. The questions do not apply to their way of life."

"Well, if 'yes' is the right answer, I got sixteen of them right. I guess I passed."

"You passed. Any doubts about your sickness?"

"Sickness? I thought I just drank too much."

"We all did, and through excessive drinking we became allergic to ethyl alcohol, which is in all liquor. We have no control over booze after the first drink."

"Is there a cure?"

"We'll never be cured," he said. "We can only arrest the disease by not drinking." He paused to penetrate, with his eyes, the fog of alcohol surrounding my mind. "One day at a time, Fred. One day at a time."

"You make it sound so simple, Scott. But you've got ten years of not drinking behind you. I'm frightened after less than two days of being dry. How am I going to handle those drinking clients who know I drank, and who I now need to get this company going? They're more important to me than they have ever been, and I don't want to turn them off by not drinking with them."

"If they're drinking a lot, Fred, the chances are they're not the big decision makers in their companies. I have found, as many others have, that the decision makers in industry are not the ones who drink heavily. There are exceptions to this, of course, but not many."

I know so little of the nondrinking world, I thought. Over the top of his raised coffee cup, Scott's eyes smiled and waited for my response. "I guess I'll have to get to know some of those dull guys who don't drink," I joked. My use of comedy to dodge an important issue did not work.

"Or else not drink with the ones you know. That's very possible," he said.

I could not cast aside the thought of my first encounter with the drinking crowd at P.J.'s. I appreciated Scott's attempt to ease my fears, but I know I must meet the ones with whom I've done so much business while going through various stages of intoxication. I told Scott I didn't know where else to begin.

"Then they're the ones you work with. But don't let them get you during these early days of being dry. When I first stopped, I lied about the reason for not drinking. I told everyone my doctor had told me to cut down for a few weeks."

"Did they believe you?"

"I don't know. Most of them didn't know I had stopped. The nonalcoholic drinker does not pay attention to how much others drink. Only the alcoholic notices others. I always wanted to be with heavy drinkers, so I watched who did the drinking, and they became my friends."

"It's amazing, Scott. That's exactly what I did. I could tell you the number of drinks each person with me had before, during, and after we ate." His blue eyes sparkled. He smiled. I'm getting the message. "I may use the medical excuse," I continued. "But before we leave, I'd like to get back to this test I just took." He waited as I finished the last of my coffee. "As I went through the questions, Scott, I kept expecting to be asked about skid row, or perhaps begging. They didn't ask if I had ever gone for an extended period of time without bathing or eating properly. They didn't even ask if I'd slept on a park bench as the result of drinking. Or had holes in my shoes. These are some questions I would have asked."

"So would I." he replied. "Guys like us would feel less like a drunk if they asked those questions. We could answer, 'no.' The truth is, Fred, that less than five percent of the more than twenty million problem drinkers in this country have ever seen skid row. Ninety-five percent are just like you and me, and a large part are women in suburbia, who are constantly protected by their families. Most problem drinkers hold jobs, have homes and families, and look quite normal to those who do not know an alcoholic. Most are successful in the eyes of society. They're difficult to spot as alcoholic."

"What are my chances of staying dry, Scott? You've seen many fail, I'm sure. Do you think I'll make it?"

"I can't answer that. And I don't think I would give you an answer even if I could. You're projecting too far ahead. Don't worry about being able to stop for the rest of your life. All you have to think about is today. You can go without a drink this afternoon. Then when you get home, don't drink before going to bed. Just handle today. This is not only my advice to you, or AA's advice to you—it's God's."

"Where'd you find that?" I questioned sharply.

"Check the Sermon on the Mount. In Matthew. I believe it's toward the end of chapter six, or in the beginning of seven. Christ tells us not to be anxious about tomorrow—to live today."

At home I searched Matthew for Scott's reference. Matthew 6:34 became the first Bible text I tried to put to memory. "So don't be anxious about tomorrow. God will take care of your tomorrow too. Live one day at a time." Christ saw me coming two thousand years ago. I almost missed him. Then he gave me the mornings.

I set about to live one day at a time. I launched each day by rising at five-thirty, with the undisguised objective of reading, and thus discovering more of Christ.

It's easier to get up early now that I'm not drinking. The last six months have tested my determination to continue this quest for a deeper relationship with God. After heavy drinking, five-thirty is the middle of the night. I've come home at that hour. Some mornings I did not make the call to the firmness of purpose I had the previous day. I could not get up. And it would not be a good day from that point forward. Most calls I somehow obeyed. A force larger than drinking pushed me from bed, and I fumbled downstairs to ask forgiveness—again. And to read.

Christ's unrelenting forgiveness of my daily drinking and halfhearted efforts to find him when I could scarcely find the Bible through which he spoke is hard to understand. My resolve to change and to stay dry found strength through Christian writers whom God used to get to my dulled brain. Roy L. Smith is one of them. He wrote a meaningful statement regarding the first segment of the day. "Psychologists are agreed and experience supports the conclusion that the first twenty minutes of the morning are of the utmost importance for the entire day. The spirit with which we greet the beginning of the day will have much to do with the way the whole day goes, and with the mood in which we come home at night. Good start, good day! Bad start, bad day!"[11] I already knew how to start bad days. I needed some good ones. Yet I could not remove myself from circumstances of easy drinking. I felt forced to seek new business through lunch, with the men around whom I had become an alcoholic. I made a lunch date with Don Andrews.

I saw six of them sitting at the bar. Only two, Don Andrews and Pat Johnson from Chicago, were my guests. The others did not have business lunches going. I deposited my overcoat, scarf, and boots with the hatcheck girl. Slush-clogged street corners made the wearing of boots wise today, but they quickly became hot when worn indoors. I disliked them immensely, except for today. I used taking them off to stall, just a little longer, my entrance into the bar.

Don Andrews and his visitor from Chicago were well into martinis. One week has passed since I drank anything alcoholic. Records are already being shattered. I have gone seven days without a drink. I have never gone through one lunch in this restaurant with these men without a drink. They have been my license for escape from myself and my guilts. Now they are Armageddon. So prolonged.

I walked to the bar, ready for their insistence that I begin the new year and the new job with a drink. This very familiar bar and restaurant, so friendly only weeks ago, is now hostile. Loud greetings and hearty welcomes bind me to the past. To last week. Alarmed, and fearful that I should not have entered, I feel timid. I don't feel in control. The entire scene flashed across my mind for the first time. Martini glasses grow from the bar top, like silver tulips in a bed of mahogany. Highball glasses rhythmically bound from bar to lips. A chorus of tinkling ice can be heard above the rumble. The air smells good. Very good. Alcohol is strongly present. I had never been aware of these smells before. Today they bid me come. Don and his companion bid me come. Tim, the bartender I have known for years, bids me come. He moves to fix my usual drink.

"Hold that, Tim," I said softly. "I'm very thirsty for some reason. Let me have a plain club soda first." He served it without comment. I turned to face my clients, now challengers, and spoke before they could question. "Welcome back to New York, Pat. Sure hope you had a nice holiday season in Chicago."

Pat Johnson was pleased I remembered his name. "This is a lousy time to come here. New York winters are wetter than ours. And a lot dirtier," he jabbed.

Don lowered his empty martini glass and said, "I, for one, am glad the holidays are over. It's time to get back to business, and trips out of town. Speaking of business, Fred, how do you like working for a California studio?"

"So far, it's great. They've given me full rein here to do as I please. Just bring in the business. That's where you guys come in."

He ignored my call for help. "I've heard of them before. They've been around for some time," he said while pantomiming a fresh drink to the bartender. He got his third martini. I was counting.

Deliberately, and in full view of both of them, I slid the mounting bar check in front of my club soda. Don and Pat did not appear to object, and neither commented on my choice of drink. Is my paying for theirs more important? Don said no.

"Slide that check back here, Fred," he demanded. "I'd

like to buy you a drink to begin the year and the job. Tim, fix this man a real drink. It's not often I buy, so when I do it'll be more than soda."

Poised, ready to stir my usual martini, Tim looked to me for the go-ahead sign. I shook my head. He did not understand my denial, but since it is not his practice to force drinks on customers, he stopped. Bartenders will not usually force drinks. They want people to drink, but only moderately. Drunks do not enhance the character of any bar. We know.

"Thanks for the offer, Don, but you'll have to owe me one. I'm just not feeling too good today. I'll stick to this." I raised my glass in salute.

"Okay, ole buddy, but don't say I didn't try," he boasted. "I'll get you later."

A crisis passed. I had made it through the initial onslaught—the hour before eating. This had been the time when I set the pace for the balance of my day and drank until bedtime. Instead, I took a seat at the bar and entered the small talk of Chicago's weather, Christmas bonuses, and impending trips to warmer climates. I reminded them of Southern California's warm winters. Time passed slowly. I attempted to present our company's directors. Pat knew both of them from previous Chicago work in California.

"They're both good guys, Fred. You won't have trouble selling them for shooting out there. I can't see bidding them to come all the way into New York, though. This town's loaded with good film directors. We don't need to import them from the Coast."

I told him we were going to hire a director for New York. My sales pitch on directors ended. I shifted to the beauty of our brownstone in New York, and to the scope of the financial commitment being made to Manhattan production. They were not interested. Neither was I. I desperately wanted to leave—to go somewhere, anywhere. But I'm trapped. Frightened.

To pass time, I watched drinks being mixed. Hundreds of

drinks are made in minutes. They're born into all sizes, shapes, and colors. I visually followed some of the more colorful ones to the table from which they were ordered, and learned it was impossible to match the drink to the person. My deeply conditioned habit of reaching for a drink, raising it to my mouth, followed by a drag on a cigarette, could not be changed today. Only the drink.

Six glasses of dull, tasteless club soda helped keep my hands occupied. Cigarettes do not taste as good, partially because I used them previously as a sobering agent. Today they're doing double duty—feeding one habit while softening the omission of another. Time passed very slowly. At last we sat to eat.

"You're sure quiet today, Fred," Chicago Pat said. "Is everything all right with you?"

"I'm fine, Pat. I guess I overdid during the holidays. Time to take it easy."

Don carefully placed an overflowing martini on the table. He had carried it cautiously from the bar so he did not have to wait while ordering lunch. Today I noticed his preparedness, and felt very sober when he said, "Drink enough club soda, and it'll make anybody quiet. I only drink it when I want to burp."

Pat enjoyed his remark. They laughed heartily. I joined in, but my laugh lied. This lunch is duty. A job. Although it's been fun to see these men, two hours of involvement with drinking—and not drinking—has magnified the ritual for me. I have not known the emphasis I placed upon these hours. I took for granted the exhilaration of lunch. My attitude craved it. But not today. Why? I know a few cocktails will help the boredom. Change it into a stimulating beginning to the rest of the day. And night. Yet I'm not tempted beyond my ability to resist. I do not want to drink. In a sea of alcohol I hold my breath. Do not swallow. I'm being protected as never before. Jesus Christ really works! He's not a concocted ideology of man. He's a power beyond man. He came to seek me. I didn't spend a lifetime searching for him, yet I found every bit of him and his truth simply by saying yes.

In this bar of many previous drinks for me, I don't want to drink today. Even a simple glass of wine, thought to be harmless, is not tempting. I've crossed another valley. Had another victory. I've made it through to coffee without drinking during an extremely uncomfortable lunch. How will I then cope with three or four each week if this one has been so unpleasant? Whom do I serve? And if this film company is not successful, how will I survive? Help me Lord. I'm in over my head. I'm dry but not sober. Dry is not drinking. Sober is not drinking—comfortably. I strive for true sobriety.

I never had to use the fabricated story of my doctor telling me to temporarily stop drinking. Two weeks passed before anyone else took notice of the club soda placed next to me during lunch. The other day I revealed I had not had a drink in weeks. Some accused me of lying, but none asked why I stopped. Others implicitly believed they had recently seen me with a martini. Most did not care. They only wanted the herd to remain unchanged. I know their need for guilt-free drinking is gratified in group drinking. My need is guilt-free nondrinking companions. Many moderate drinkers in advertising are unearthed as I broaden my list of prospective customers. New-fledged clients comment when I pick up bar checks and attempt to pay for their cocktail while all I have is inexpensive club soda. The scene is changing. Old drinking holes do not satisfy my new thirsts, yet I also continue to seek new business from the old group with which I no longer feel comfortable. I'm afraid to let go completely because I now have no place to hide. And I'm frustrated at not sharing Christ at lunch.

I long for Christian fellowship on this side of the Hudson. I have not been forced to give up the old life—it's become rubbish to me. Unfulfilling. These bars have become very flat. Stale. The air doesn't smell as good as it once did. The only fresh winds are felt when each morning I give my will to God and try my best to not take it back before reaching the city. I strive to put the day's outcome into his hands— to realign myself with Christ so I don't have to concern myself with the results of the day. I ask for another twenty-four hours of sobriety, and turn my fear of drinking over to him. Despite all, I trust myself more than I trust him, and continue to possess my fear of drinking as though I must keep it to myself, or lose it. Most mornings I leave Christ on the bus, or I lock him in the car in a parking lot, and question why I'm unable to witness effectively in the marketplace of cocktail lounges and advertising agencies. Consequently I actively join the small talk of lunch upon lunch. But I do not drink. I'm able to withdraw daily from the liquor to which my body impels me. Lunchtime shortens. Afternoons produce more sales calls, and advertising executives who drink moderately, or not at all, continue to build the base from which new business flows.

The abundance of new production catapulted our New York office into a profitable position three months after we opened. And I did not drink. P.J.'s seldom saw me standing at the bar. My prestige soared in the eyes of California and the three employees in our Manhattan brownstone. No one questioned my authority or leadership. We soon hired an additional film director from Hollywood and brought him and his family east. Production in Manhattan began. Scott was correct once more. It's getting better all the time. To fill the lack of Christian fellowship in my life, I recklessly offered our building as the site for weekly prayer meetings.

The historical brownstone, built before the American Revolution, on what was then farmland, became a weekly meeting place for eight born-again Manhattan businessmen. My weekly prayer partners were the president of an international magazine, an insurance broker, the national sales manager of a midwest utility conglomerate, a Wall Street broker, and one of the most successful hair stylists in town. From dodging cars in Brooklyn and on

Forty-second Street to getting on my knees each week with these men—the contrast affirmed another of God's miracles.

The steel and concrete "farmland" outside our prayer circle added to the uniqueness of our meetings. Open prayers, in the heart of New York's urgent business life, were nourished through Arline's gracious ministry of traveling into the City to prepare unforgettable lunches for us. For the first time, I joined lunches which were not on an expense account. And no one drank. None of these men who meet are clients of ours, hence I could not use the rationale of helping business by consenting to the use of our offices for prayer.

Our three employees had considerable trouble relating to eight Christian men arriving on our doorstep each week. These men came dressed in handsome business suits. Some carried attaché cases, made quick phone calls before the meeting, and resembled prosperous leaders in their fields. When informed by me of the positions held by my Christian brothers, our staff could not link together titles and prayers. They quickly identified the group as "your friends," or "another one." A much-used announcement of arrivals developed. "Someone has just walked to the back of the building. He's smiling, so he must be one of yours." We were witnessing through our joy. God blessed us with more business.

California reacted by presenting me with a new Mercedes-Benz sedan, and requested I come west with a new insurance company production God gave us through one of my new, nondrinking, clients. I squeamishly accepted the travel offer.

Newark Airport, the scene of many previous drinks and innumerable flights never made, bustled with activity. The main terminal, jammed with faceless people, all going somewhere, offered instant anonymity. I felt it at once. The chance of meeting a familiar face in the crowd is extremely low. The chance of drinking very high, particularly as my flight to California is late. It will not leave for over an hour. I'm alone in an ocean of people who do not know me. Or my problem. Or fear. I not only have time to drink before getting on board the airplane, I have time to sober up once safely and securely locked inside the jet. And if I do drink on the flight across country, I'll have time tonight to dry out before meeting my bosses tomorrow morning. I used this logic many times. It always worked before.

Today is no different. I'm free of all responsibilities, relationships, and judgments. I have a good job, expense cash in my wallet, and valid credit cards. Each supports the feeling of taking one harmless drink to help pass the hour. No one will know. I've been dry for almost three months. Perhaps I've learned my lesson. I've proved I can go without booze. Could I control drinking now? I saw an empty phone stall.

Bill Reynolds is a very successful salesman. He does a lot of traveling. He's also an alcoholic. A recovering alcoholic with more than twelve years of sobriety. When I heard Bill speak recently, his drunk story was my story. Credit cards, expense accounts, and success. All of it. He also lives in New Jersey, so I asked him to be my sponsor. My advisor. He gave me his business card and assured me I could call anytime. Now was the time.

"Bill, I'm sorry to bother you at work, but I'm sure glad you are in. I need your help."

"You've got it, Fred. Where are you calling from?"

"Newark Airport. I'm on my way to California. My first time since being dry."

"And you're stuck at the airport with nothing to do."

"Right. As a matter of fact, my flight has been delayed for over an hour, and I'm concerned about drinking."

"Airports are the greatest places in the world for drinking. I know. Have you had a drink yet?"

"No, I haven't. And that's why I called. I have thoughts of taking one—that it wouldn't hurt to have just one to kill some time."

"It could kill you," he said. "Do you really feel like the drink, or is it just to be doing what you've always done at airports?"

"That's probably part of it," I confessed. "I always drink when I'm on the road. Particularly at airports. I love them." I tried to make it seem so normal.

"Well, go and have a drink, then," he said.

His suggestion completely surprised me. Took me off guard. I expected—wanted—to be convinced not to drink. Is Bill really just like those drinking clients who don't care if I drink? My silence told him more than I knew.

"Fred, I can't stop you from drinking if that's what you want. You're the only one who can control that. Some of us have to go back to it—to the gutter again—before we really reach bottom. I slipped twice before finally realizing I could not have that first drink. Even at airports." He paused, then hit me again. "You may not be ready for sobriety." He made his statement. He's being honest, and tough. With love.

"I think I am ready for sobriety. Bill. I'm just having a time of it here not knowing what to do with myself."

"Don't get me wrong," he said. "I sure don't want you to take a drink. I only want you to know that if you do drink on this trip, and then want to come back to sobriety, give me a call and we'll try again."

"Damn you, Bill. You know I don't want to start over. I'll get some coffee and read one of the books I've got with me."

"Great. Just don't drink until you get on the plane. Then don't drink until you get to California. One day, or one minute at a time, Fred. Break it down into sizes you can see."

"Okay," I replied. "I'll be fine now."

"Before you go, let me give you a tip for the airplane. The very first time a stewardess asks you if you'd like a drink, don't just refuse the drink. Tell her you do not drink. That you can't drink. It usually stops further asking."

"Okay, Bill. I'll try it your way," I promised.

"I'll be praying for you, Fred. You're going to be just fine. Get some coffee and a candy bar. And stop projecting. I'll see you when you get back. God bless you."

"Thanks for being around. I'll be thinking about what you've said." I hung up and looked for a bar. A snack bar.

Once on board, and airborne, I felt more in control. Drinking coffee and reading during the waiting time gave me confidence. I felt I could abstain for the duration of the cross-country flight. The thought of one week in California, with clients out from New York, troubled me. Even if they didn't drink heavily. Lunches during pre-production, and dinners out most every night, are normal functions. The night lights of Hollywood summon men from their normal behavior. The three-hour time differential puts their families on the East Coast in bed when it's only nine o'clock in the evening in California. Phone calls home have been made. Freedom from being questioned regarding where, with whom, and how late, promotes excitement about going "out on the town." On an expense account. With company credit cards. Money and time, normal problems at home, become the prime reason for not staying home. Hotel rooms are for times of exhaustion. When there's nothing else to do. When it's getting close to tomorrow. I'm curious about my new reaction to repetitive nights of merrymaking. Has it ever been done on club soda? And lime?

Soon after landing at Los Angeles International Airport, I found the reserved rental car. The San Diego freeway pointed me toward Hollywood. In serious need of help now that I've arrived, I spoke to God as I drove. I asked for guidance, and the knowledge that he is with me. He answered. Or is it coincidence when my most favorite hymn bursts forth on the radio of a strange automobile as I touch the first station selector? Someone before me had preset a local Christian station to the one button I pushed. John Newton's immortal declaration in "Amazing Grace" brought tears as I sang along joyously with the radio choristers. The lyrics of the verse I first heard tonight told me exactly what would happen to me in California: "Through many dangers, toils and snares, I have already come; 'tis grace hath brought be safe thus far, and grace will lead me home."

"Thank you, Lord. Thank you, Lord," I shouted. No one in other cars on this busy ten-lane highway heard my thanks. My praise. I felt a cleansing, as though the silent passenger of former lonely drives decided he would leave.

The millions of beckoning lights of sprawling Los Angeles do not frighten as much as they did only moments ago. I checked the hour. There's still time to call the central office of Alcoholics Anonymous. "California AA, here I come," I shouted. "I'm going to make it, Lord. I'm going to make it tonight. You want me at an AA meeting this first night, then that's where I'll be. Thank you Lord, for telling me so quickly." His grace, through AA, protected my delicate gift of sobriety throughout the first day and night in Hollywood. I prepared to meet this town, and visiting clients, one day at a time. The next day began early. Immediately after breakfast I received a call from Peter Stockton, the agency film producer for this insurance job.

"I've purposely taken a large suite, Fred, so we can hold a few meetings right here in the hotel. The bar is stocked and room service will bring hors d'oeuvres to hold us until dinner. So how about five this evening?" My heart beat faster as he continued. "Our insurance client is here, the account guy is with him, and our agency creative chief even came out for the shoot. We're going to have a time of it."

Peter Stockton, a new client for me, and a man with whom I have done little drinking, seems prepared for a party. I don't need a party. I need strength to not drink today. Yesterday's flight out here, the miracle of the Christian radio station, and the tremendous AA meeting, kept me from drinking. Now I must go to this meeting tonight. And I must take these men to dinner. To drinks before dinner. I have no other choice.

I easily found Peter's suite. It was located poolside. I had passed it enroute to my own room yesterday. We had all chosen the same hotel to simplify meetings and rendez-vous. It also simplified drinking together. He left his door ajar, signaling entrance without knocking. I walked in un-announced.

Three men leaned on the small, well stocked bar in Pe-ter's living room as I walked in. I did not know how to handle this predicament. As introductions were being made, Peter answered the ringing phone. Before being positioned to announce my drink preference, Peter inter-rupted. "That was the front desk, Fred. A telegram has just arrived for you."

The cavalry again. I wonder who's leading the attack this time.

"You guys continue," I suggested. "I'll be right back."

Every time I receive a telegram I initially feel it's be-cause the person sending it has not been able to make contact through others means, and in his frustration, has resorted to the telegram. At least the effort to get through is thus recorded. I was wrong. This wire carried life.

"Fred, our brother in Christ: From New York to Califor-nia we wing our prayers each day, that you may be led by the Lord, strengthened by the Lord, and protected by the Lord. We are with you in spirit, so don't let anyone or anything divert you from your cause or your witness. Hurry home. We all love you." It was signed, "The Monday lunch bunch."

I choked up. Tears formed. I walked out to the pool area. Under a tree. I thanked God for his message of encourage-ment. His presence. His precise timing. Fear of drinking vanished.

I turned toward Peter's room and a night in Hollywood.

*The great thing
in the world
is not so much
where we stand,
as in what direction
we are moving.*
OLIVER WENDELL
HOLMES[12]

9

SITUATION HOPELESS
BUT NOT SERIOUS

The most substantial martini I had ever ordered came to a stop directly in front of me. A chorus of suppressed desires sounded from within my head. Saliva glands awakened taste buds long kept in check.

I cannot recall how I came upon this tranquil cocktail lounge. I sat isolated before a massive glass-top bar, resplendent in its cleanness. A soft white light came from beneath. It heightened the purity of the commanding liquid before me, and cast an unearthly reflection from row upon row of whiskey bottles posted at attention against the back wall. I could not divert my eyes from the captivating potion before me. Its long crystal stem sparkled. Its V-shaped bowl frosted, obviously frozen before the gin and vermouth joined in composing the most perfectly mixed narcotic known. A submerged olive, large as a walnut, lay in wait for its final moment. Its wrinkled skin revealed its Greek origin.

In one swift, gluttonous act, I drank the total contents of

the inviting concoction and knew instantly the damage done.

Six months of sobriety—of being dry—gone. Gone, too, the victories during flights to California and other places without succumbing. Hundreds of hours of standing sober before bars throughout New York City while clients drank their minds away—all this lay wasted. One hundred eighty guilt-free days of proudly accounting for each minute are irretrievable.

Remorse. Guilt. Shame. Failure. All strike simultaneously. There are no thoughts of why I slipped. I hurt too much. How, or in what mode of being I departed, I cannot remember. Upon opening my eyes the next morning, I knew I had to take action. Immediately. There must be an explanation for this shocking crisis. Does it imply these first months of abstinence are meaningless?

"Of course not, Fred," Bill Reynolds laughed boldly. "That's not an unusual dream for us." My sponsor's six feet five inches towered above me. I looked up as he continued. "Most recovering alcoholics dream about drinking from time to time. I still do, and they're still nightmares. But they remind me of how fortunate I am that I always wake up sober. That I really didn't have a drink. So don't you spend time worrying about the dream. You didn't drink."

This wise and experienced counselor, my AA sponsor, again set me free. I dropped the ugly dream, held to the fear of that first drink, and each day gained more serenity.

Change continued. Slowly. Gradually.

I set out to let go of yesterdays as never before. I looked forward to the day discovered each morning with Christ. To the release of my instinctive impulses to drink. He took them, along with my will, and in exchange, offered a deep personal relationship. I seized his offers cheerfully, then struggled to keep alive the awareness that I have the willpower to set the quality of my life. To choose my way or his way. I became conscious of a higher standard from which to model each period of my life. A gradual metamorphosis emerged. The repugnant past seemed less ponderous, and I didn't have to live back there. Today is one more fresh moment in which to acknowledge Christ's lordship. With all my imperfections, my new birthright is God's viewpoint of me through Jesus Christ. Not as I see myself. Or as anyone else sees me.

Paul, in his letter to the church at Philippi, may have had a like discovery when he wrote, "I don't mean to say I am perfect. I haven't learned all I should even yet, but I keep working toward that day when I will finally be all that Christ saved me for and wants me to be" (Phil. 3:12). But Paul wasn't a television commercial film producer. He didn't have California infringing upon his ministry. Or a company president at his tent flap, telling him how to make tents.

Nine months of consuming work spawned our thriving New York subsidiary. It also attracted John Alexander, our president in Hollywood. In one person, he is also a partner and the corporation attorney. New to the film profession, this native Californian came to the mecca of television advertising decisions to seek his fortune. And change mine. He came with his Mercedes-Benz, his wife, and two children. They soon settled in a fashionable apartment overlooking the East River. His children enrolled in private schools. The thriving, subservient New York branch paid all expenses. Our overhead costs soared. John Alexander looked for ways to cut costs. He found eight men in his dining room. And no clients.

"Who are those men downstairs, Fred?"

"They're friends of mine, John. They're all very successful businessmen in their respective fields." He was not impressed.

"Are any of them clients of ours? And if not, what are they doing here?"

"Months ago I mentioned to you, during one of our phone conversations, that I conducted a nonbusiness luncheon here every week. You didn't object to it then."

"I must have had heavier things on my mind as well as

being far removed in California. What are you meeting here for?" he repeated.

"These are some of the men I met during a special weekend retreat in upstate New York. We meet each week to share experiences—to see if we can help each other with the job of living as God wants us to live." I watched his expression.

Bewildered, he said, "I know you're a religious man, Fred, and I think it's great that men in this city meet from time to time to do whatever it is you do when you meet. But this building is for business only. That room in which you're meeting and eating is for client use. The kitchen is to prepare client lunches, so we can save money by entertaining here. That's one of the reasons we took the place."

"Are you telling me you want me to stop today's meeting?"

"It's too late for that, now. But I do feel you should make other arrangements for next Monday. I really don't want them held here." He looked chagrined. "I have no objection to religion, Fred. I was brought up in the church. I just never got into it deeply, and I don't think it can be mixed with business. It belongs on Sunday."

I could not cast the first stone. But I picked one up. "It certainly hasn't hurt business."

"It's not helping when it occupies time of our staff and uses space intended for other use. More important, you are not out with a prospective client today. One fifth of your five weekly lunch days is not being used effectively for this company. I absolutely want you to take the meeting out of here. It's creating too much confusion."

"That's okay, John. If we're to meet in another place, it's because there's good reason for it. I accept that." I turned to the stairwell leading down. "This will be the last one," I smiled. He shook his head and turned for a telephone.

I extinguished the lone candle around which we had prayed. This last Monday lunch in the brownstone came to an end. We prayed for everyone in the building, and asked

God's richest blessing upon our evictor from California. We believed another portion of the already-crowded air space in this city had been reserved for us. Our prayers created excitement regarding God's planning. His answer came through a young priest of St. Thomas Episcopal Church on Fifth Avenue. One of our members had met with the young clergyman weeks ago for other purposes. During that encounter, our Monday conclaves were made known and an offer for a room in the spacious, sharing, midtown church was extended. We quickly accepted the invitation.[13]

Each Monday I enter the same tiny elevator in which Scott Campbell and I rode to my first AA meeting almost nine months ago. Occasionally Scott, and an unknown recovering alcoholic, ride with me. The alcoholic alights at the third floor amidst the noise and laughter which is AA. Brown bags of lunch in hand, Scott and I continue to the fifth floor. To our retreat. During each short ride I'm reminded of the Lord's keen ability to impress certain truths on us. For as long as I attend this prayer meeting, in this church, a piece of me goes to that third-floor room in which his power for me was made manifest in Alcoholics Anonymous.

Fellowship with this "Monday lunch bunch" helped me to begin to grasp the incredible gift of God seeing me without sin. He has forgotten all I've done! He sees me perfect because he sees me first through Christ. And then forgets. I can't see me as perfect. And I have trouble forgetting. I remember too much of the hurting past, which continues to give me reservations about my ability to control the future.

I lose sight of his promise to provide all my needs—not my wants. I read somewhere that if I can get my "wants" closer to my "needs," I'll be a rich man. First I'll have to identify needs beyond the physical food, clothing, and shelter minimum needs. I want freedom from financial instability, yet cannot bring myself to fully trust God for its solution. In fact, I do not fully trust God for the fulfillment of anything for which I have always been responsible. I simply have not trusted God. So I prayed daily that I would be shown how to trust him more. The Teacher heard my prayer. He used circumstances I created to present gifts no other kingdom could purchase. When all financial support vanished, he appeared. I finally recognized him right in the middle of defeat. What a victory!

Ownership of the Fifth Avenue specialty shop for which Arline worked passed to new ownership with whom she did not feel comfortable. The new regime also created an atmosphere in which Arline felt a confined future. Inasmuch as alcohol no longer invaded our fears, and my position in New York's film community had the semblance of being secure, she risked her financial independence on a sober alcoholic and his feeble attempts to improve. Her resignation, from a world in which she received outstanding recognition and acclaim, affirmed her love and support. Thus encouraged, I firmly grasped the reins as spiritual head of our household and restlessly searched for daily clues to the Lord's leading. Unable to recognize positive clues, I made my own. Then I tailored them to fit my need. Even on Third Avenue. In the rain.

Empty taxi cabs become nonexistent on the streets of Manhattan when it's raining. Today's cold November rain filled every public vehicle I could see. I have a meeting one hour from now. The advertising agency, which called for our sample reel of commercials produced recently, also asked me to bring our resident director to their screening and subsequent bidding session. The forty-seven-storied Post Office building, which houses their offices, stands directly across the street. My first call this wet morning, in another skyscraper close by, ended later than planned. The downpour, and taxi problem, has stranded me. At this hour I'd be late returning to the meeting for which I'm an hour early, if I don't move. I didn't move. I planted myself in the Post Office building coffee shop, leaving an elevator ride between me and my next appointment. I had an unexpected, free hour to myself.

I welcomed unforeseen time now. These periods no longer breed fear of waiting without drinking. Vacant time has become a friend. I enjoy it in company with writers, who have come to me during one year of reading their works. Exciting challenges have been opened through inspiring lives of others who have chosen to be led by God into the service of leading others to him. Edith Schaeffer is one of these exciting people.

Her dynamic book *L'Abri* planted a seed of radical change. Her account of God's power and dependability set me on fire. I envied the Schaeffers. In my mind, they had experienced the ideal escape. As I read about their mountain retreat in Switzerland, and the miracles they have lived, I longed to get out of New York City. To chuck the film business. Forget advertising agencies. Stop commuting. Especially in the rain. I dreamed of opening a new retreat center in New Jersey. One dedicated to Christ, of course, and to the work of introducing men and women to him. Or, one geared to the needs of young people. Or to newly married. To alcoholics. Wayward teenagers. Anyone and everyone. I only wanted to witness where it would matter, where there are lost souls. To frightened and insecure people. During my third cup of coffee I asked God to show me the way into service. I focused my prayers on an obscure mountain in New Jersey, while I sat on the most densely populated island of lost souls in our country. And I thought I heard his call. Arline thought she heard the same call.

"If we ever go into the retreat business, Fred, we've got our first piece of cooking equipment." Before I could get my raincoat unbuttoned, Arline slid a forty-gallon aluminum pot across the kitchen floor. The mountain looked closer. What's the English word for L'Abri?

"Where in the world did you get that?" I shouted.

"You'll never guess," she joked. "So I'll tell you."

I raised the lid of the largest cooking pot I had ever seen.

Arline's voice became excited. "I was at church today, helping with the bazaar that's coming up in two days. I told you about it. Anyhow, I was in the church basement with another woman. We were getting some old items together for sale at the bazaar. I picked up this huge pot, and asked how much it was going to sell for. The woman told me to put my own price on it, to make an offer. At this point, I told her it would make a dandy pot for our retreat house and that we could cook enough spaghetti in it to feed an army. She told me if it was going to be used for the Lord's work, it was mine for no charge. So I took it as coming from the Lord."

"Honey, I don't believe what you're telling me." My smile triggered her face. Her eyes sparkled in anticipation of an obvious conclusion to the incident. "I prayed on Third Avenue today. Now you know I've done many things on Third Avenue in my time, but today is the first time I've prayed."

"I can just imagine what you've done on Third Avenue," she hinted.

"Score one for you," I nodded, and accordingly gave her an account of my morning delay and coffee shop prayer. "The Lord is telling us what he wants us to do with our lives," I concluded.

"Maybe he wants us to go to Africa with our pot," she punned. "Or are we to open a soup kitchen in Hoboken?" Before I could reply, she continued her joy. "Ken and Ann could serve tables and I could handle the money. You can do the cooking."

I enjoyed her humor. "Very funny, Arline, but I did pray for guidance regarding my feelings about going into a retreat center. I think he's telling us something when you bring home a pot this size the very day I prayed for direction. This monstrous kettle is certainly not for our small kitchen."

"Do you think you'll quit your job tomorrow?" she snickered.

"You're joking, but if I had enough money I probably would. I do know if the Lord wants us in retreat work, that's where we're going to be. Not only will we feel at peace about going in that direction, but nothing will stop us from getting there. Not even our lack of money. Or your jokes."

"I know that, Fred." She put her hand on my arm. "I'm happy because we're both looking for God's direction. I'm not alone anymore. Just to hear you speaking the way you are tonight is enough of a miracle for me. I can remember, so well, how I wanted you to speak of Christ with me. Now you do it easily. Since you stopped drinking, the Lord has really come into your life."

"I'm sure glad you stayed around all these years, honey. I don't know why you did, but I praise God every day for your being here," I said.

Silent a moment before speaking, she said, "I didn't have much choice most of those years, Fred. Where could I have taken Ann and Ken? I didn't want to go back to Missouri, and I couldn't support them on my own. You had us trapped."

"We had lots of good times," I suggested. "Our marriage hasn't been all bad for you and the kids. Has it?"

"Some of it was too good," she said with devastating calmness. "But you're right. We have always had fun together. And I guess I stayed through the drinking and suspicions because you have always been kind to me and the children, even though I have been hurt by your attention to other women and your need to drink before your need for me or your family."

Guilty as charged! And forgiven.

"But I'm beginning to understand more of your disease, Fred. Alanon tells me you drank because you had no choice. As difficult as it is for me to fully understand that, I must believe it's the reason for the past, and that God has put things in place of drinking which are more than substitutes for it."

"Thank you for those feelings, honey. I hope you're right. All I know is that I used to worry about what I would do

with the time I'd have available if I did stop drinking. Now
I'm so busy I don't know where I'd get the time to drink."

"Yes, I know," she replied. "For almost eleven months
now, I've watched you becoming involved. You've spent
weekends in New York State cooking for other men's
weekends and on the team speaking. You've been responsible for pushing the first such men's weekend for New Jersey. Most every night is taken with activity away from
home."

"I'm sorry, honey."

"No, you don't understand. I'm not complaining about
you being away so much because it's keeping you sober. I
guess its your medicine. Many women find their alcoholic
partner out as much and more than when he drank. We
know it's helpful, even though we'd like to know how to
keep you guys at home, drunk or sober. Maybe a retreat
center would at least give us the chance to work closer."

"I really feel positive about today, Arline. The Lord is
getting us prepared for something exciting, and I must tell
you, I'm beginning to feel his involvement more each day.
Even at work."

"Based on what you've been telling me about the studio,
business has been good. I suppose they're happy back in
California."

"I'm not sure, honey. John's there now, and I haven't
been told the purpose. We've not had a new job awarded to
us for about a month. Ever since we were forced to stop our
Monday meetings. I'm trying very hard to really trust the
Lord for the lack of business and the sudden insecurity I'm
feeling, particularly since John came to New York."

We each realized I was projecting into many tomorrows,
and that I would be wise to wait until I heard from California. I heard.

"We're not going to use company credit cards anymore,
Fred," John said. I thought I detected coolness in his voice,
but credited it to the telephone connection between New
York and Los Angeles. "I'll be back tomorrow afternoon,"
he continued. "I have a check for you for five hundred

dollars and one for myself in the same amount. You and I can use this as our base for personal petty cash. When we see it getting low, we submit expense reports and accounting back here will bring us up to the original five hundred."

"Sounds good to me, John, but why no cards?"

"They're getting out of hand. Not necessarily from New York, but our crews have been using them for location shoot expenses. Hotels, meals, and airline tickets create staggering bills. So we've gone on a cash basis."

I did not associate this tactic with a money problem. Business for this first year had been good. Where are the profits going? And why has California been so late in paying New York bills? Our paychecks are good. Only one had not cleared my bank in New Jersey. John assured me he had failed to transfer money quickly enough. He apologized for the mistake. This personal petty cash account may be a blunder also. Our clients will silently question the use of cash for lunch. Credit cards are a most visible measure of wealth. And credit ratings. They're also less intimidating to lunch guests. Plastic doesn't feel as much like real money.

John returned to New York as scheduled. We met after four o'clock on Thursday. He gave me my five-hundred-dollar check. I deposited it in our account the next morning before commuting back to the city. I looked forward to this Friday in Manhattan. The holiday season is upon us. In two weeks Thanksgiving will usher in the most festive five weeks of the entire year, and I will face my first full year of not tasting alcohol in any form. Those alcohol-induced dreams of Saturdays past are slowly becoming reality. One third of the dream is in existence. Increased income and significant savings will draw near if I don't draw alcohol. I considered the conflict with booze finished only at the close of each day. John Alexander did battle at the beginning of the day.

He intercepted me before I reached my desk. "I'm glad you got in a little early, Fred. I'd like to meet with you downstairs. Now, if you would."

"I'm on my way. Just let me take this coat off and pick up

a cup of coffee." I thought he might be thinking of returning to the West Coast now that he's tasted a little cold
weather. Or has he noticed the coincidence of business to
our prayer meetings? Certainly not.

I entered the downstairs living room, the "chapel" in
which we had felt the presence of the Holy Spirit. I didn't
feel him now. I felt alone. John Alexander was in the room.
He looked alone, back turned, hands clasped behind. He
rubbed them together nervously. He lowered his head for a
moment before turning. Then he stood straight, bracing
himself for the haste with which he spoke.

"It's not working out between us, Fred. We're calling an
end to our association with New York and therefore with
you." He sighed. I felt relief come over him as he sat heavily into the stuffed leather-covered divan. I sat on the other
end of the same piece of furniture. I could not believe his
declaration.

"John, this is crazy. Do you mean to tell me, that between last night at four o'clock, when you gave me a check
for five hundred dollars in petty cash, and this morning,
you guys have decided to close this office? What happened
overnight? From the looks of you, you didn't get too much
sleep.

He shook his head. "I didn't, I can assure you. This is not
easy, Fred."

"Well, I guess it isn't. Furthermore, I don't see how you
can just announce I'm no longer with the company even if
you are closing. I'm a stockholder with a three-year contract with you guys. You're the one who engineered the
deal."

"I know that, and you know the contract is with the New
York corporation and doesn't mean a thing. So is your stock.
There's not much you can do."

"I guess I'll have to sue."

"Go right ahead, but I can tell you we have the right to
dissolve this company as we choose, and there's not much

you can do about it. We're really sorry, but this is our decision."

I stood. He followed my lead. I thought of L'Abri and the forty-gallon aluminum pot in our basement. "There's a good reason for all of this, John. I really believe that, so I'm not worried about my future. It's in God's hands, as I have believed this company has been in his hands."

"When you talk like that, Fred, I have trouble looking you in the eye. I can't comprehend your reaction to what's just happened."

"Look at me now, John," I charged. Our eyes met. "I'm really sorry this has happened. But not for me, John. I'm concerned about you. It's obvious you don't like what you're into. You appear to be running scared. I'm not scared, John."

"I know you're not. There's something about you that I can't control, and there's also a confidence in your face I didn't expect. I can't get into God the way you are, even though it seems to work for you."

"He works, John. He works. And because he does, we're going to be OK. As I said before, I don't always know how he works. I only know that God is. And that's all I need."

I knew there was little I could do about the breach of contract. I also knew I did not have to take a drink because of this bizarre development. A spiritual intoxication took hold of me. I eagerly looked forward to the Lord's guiding and did not attempt to anticipate tomorrow. I could not help wondering how we were going to survive without income, but I did not question that we would survive.

The Mercedes-Benz had to be turned back to the leasing company in one week. John and I agreed to a fifteen-hundred-dollar settlement, which cancelled the contract and cleared me of any indebtedness to them. The only enigma to our pressing need for cash came when John told me I would not receive the termination money until after the first of the year. And they had put a stop-payment order on the expense check deposited this morning. I phoned every member of the "Monday lunch bunch." The cavalry faced its most difficult assignment.

My announcement of being fired visibly shook Dale Sheffield. Dale, who had been used by the Lord to get me to the weekend retreat eighteen months ago, who had heard me give my life to Christ that unforgettable rainy Sunday, and who had witnessed my growth in the Spirit, could not easily accept my new hardship.

"What in the world are you going to do, Fred?" he asked. "And right before Thanksgiving and Christmas."

"I honestly don't know, Dale. But the Lord knows. So I'm going to have to rely on him to lead the way. I'm certainly going to begin looking around immediately, and pray that he guides me to the right place, at the right time. He knows what's happened."

Prayer and support engulfed me. The lunch bunch became the twenty-ninth chapter of the Book of Acts, written for today. I know, without doubt, that God is leading. These brothers in faith did not let go of me. They affirmed God's promises and showed me his grace once more. They led me to Second Corinthians 4:8, 9. "We are pressed on every side by troubles, but not crushed and broken. We are perplexed because we don't know why things happen as they do, but we don't give up and quit. We are hunted down, but God never abandons us. We get knocked down, but we get up again and keep going." I knew I would get up again, and keep going. Somehow. But I didn't know how my family would react. I underestimated Arline, Ann, and Ken.

"I've been fired." Three words never before put together and applied to me. They stung Arline with their finality. We went into the living room. She had set a fire. The warm room and burning oak logs struck me as possessions of a suddenly deceased loved one. They did not belong with events of the day.

"How could they have done that to you?" she asked.

Then moving closer, she looked innocent to the next step of
our lives. "What are we going to do?" Before I could respond, she continued, "This is a first for us. You've never
been fired before. You've left companies, but they've never
left you." She took my hand. "My deepest concern, Fred,
is not that you've been fired. It's for you. Are you all right?"

"Yes, I'm fine, honey. Just very surprised that it happened. And that it came without any warning. There's got
to be more to it than letting me go. They're in some kind of
financial trouble on the Coast I would guess."

"I don't know what kind of trouble that puts us in, Fred,
but I can certainly go back to work, and I'm sure you'll get
another studio job quickly. But how are we going to pay this
month's bills and keep Ann in school?"

"I don't know, hon. We're okay for money until the first
of December. Then we'll be completely broke. We've got
less than six hundred in the bank, and I still must pay Ann's
tuition for November."

She appeared resigned to the facts, then said, "A lot can
happen in two weeks." She was interrupted by our front
door chimes. Dale Sheffield entered. He came directly
from the city without first going home. He looked very
worried.

"I'm really upset about you being fired today, Fred." He
turned to Arline. "I can't believe it. Not to you two. You've
been through enough, and then when everything was going
along nicely, this. Now what are you going to do?"

"Why don't you sit down and have a drink?" I asked.
Then, in response to his surprise, I said, "No, not me,
Dale. I have no intention of drinking over this." I felt Ar-
line's hand find mine. "But that's no reason why you and
Arline can't have one if you wish. It won't bother me in the
least."

He had a drink, and shook his head repeatedly while
saying, "Cheeze." Gaining control of his loss for other
words, he repeated, "I don't believe it. Not to you two. It's
so unfair. And at this time of the year." I thought he would

cry. He wanted so much to help, to support us by enduring the initial shock of the day with us. To share our loss. His anxiety for our predicament demanded action.

"Now listen, both of you," he asserted. "I know you must return that expensive car soon, so you'll be without transportation. My mother just gave us her nine-year-old Buick. It runs like a fine Swiss watch, so now we have three cars. We don't need three cars. In fact, we can't even drive three cars, so the Lord must have this one in mind for you until you get another job. Don't tell us you won't take it, because it was a gift to us and it's now a gift to you. Keep it as long as you wish." Then, "Cheeze."

It has always been difficult for me to receive. Dale made it easier. And the Lord showed his hand in our day-to-day living. We had been placed on a precipice, with no one in New York willing to throw us a rope until January.

The approach of Thanksgiving and Christmas ignites the City's most festive mood. Fifth Avenue resembles a mall. The attitude is holiday. Everywhere. Manhattan is an island of lights. One bright copywriter said, "It's the whispering time of the year." It's also the heavy drinking time. Parties and extra long lunches will not tempt me this year. I need not have worried about how to not drink in New York during this time of absolution for drunks. Every adversity does have its benefits. And questions.

Are we, I wondered, being positioned to know poverty in preparation for retreat work? Is privation necessary that we may better serve? Does Ann leave Hood College for full-time employment? Ken must complete high school. The house has already been remortgaged. How much more can I get out of it if we're forced to sell? Where will we move? During Christmas. And my first birthday in AA.

I do not know the answers today. I know they will come because I'm not afraid to seek, to knock, and to ask. This precipice is where he will use me. I had prayed that I might know how to trust him more. He's answering that prayer, dramatically.

Although all human resources have been denied us, I know he does not intend we suffer and fall. He allows me to bring those circumstances into play which I have created through my own decisions, but he does not purposely trip me to teach me how to walk. His Word and his promises support my faltering steps.

"Even though the fig trees are all destroyed, and there is neither blossom left nor fruit, and though the olive crops all fail, and the fields lie barren; even if the flocks die in the fields and the cattle barns are empty, yet I will rejoice in the Lord; I will be happy in the God of my salvation" (Hab. 3:17, 18).

If nightmares of drinking can encourage sobriety, misfortune can certainly encourage trusting.

From where I stand, I can only move in one direction.

*Life is
not a search
for happiness.
Happiness is a
by-product of
living the right
kind of life.*
ANONYMOUS

10

CHRIST IS NOT
A HEADHUNTER

Twenty-three restless, pliable humans beings trailed in line ahead of me. Each probed for their turn before window "A to K," the well from which will flow our only money until a job is found.

I counted those before me to estimate the time it will take to become number one, to stand before someone who cares about my desperate financial condition. Someone to act on our behalf. I miscalculated my arrival at "A to K" by thirty minutes. Collecting money for not working involves work. And patience. I had prayed for both.

"Applications forms are at window three," she said without emotion.

"Not here?"

"Not here. Window three. Next."

In less than one hour, I learned where to begin this function of procuring money without employment. Other lessons have taken longer for me to master. Some were more painful. More costly. None were more humbling.

Seeking unemployment compensation is upsetting enough without the added embarrassment of being rejected by an unfamiliar person who didn't care about my circumstances. Or give me enough time to impress upon her that I have never had to come to this crossroad before today. A faceless person behind me promptly smothered the window as I turned to find the starting point in this apparently endless room of wall-to-wall people.

Those in line in back of me proudly showed their completed application forms. They looked at me, then their finished paper work. They smiled without parting lips. Hostile body language separated us. I felt singled out as a foreigner invading territory familiar to them only. I'm out of my normal neighborhood. In their environment. Memories of straying into treacherous Brooklyn borderlands flourished. The full-length leather coat I wore added to my sense of not belonging. It paraded money before the line, when our common lack of income should be our bond to equality. Instead I feel most conspicuous. But not enough to run. Not this time. God's exciting, although unknown, plans kept me from bolting. Thus, I submitted to their processing and their many questions. I watched my infant dossier grow in weight.

My mother's maiden name and her place of birth were more important than military service. I thought they'd show special consideration to a former Air Force pilot. An officer. I could have shown combat ribbons. They didn't ask. They only wanted to make certain I qualified for my present position—unemployed. I qualified. Easily.

Now the State of New Jersey will provide food money. I had successfully completed application for aid. When I presented myself at window "A to K" in fourteen days I'd receive my first check for two weeks of not working. I'll be here. Dressed casually. Appearing more in need so I won't feel so out of place just two days before Christmas. I wondered if they were going to decorate this drab place. Arline had our home trimmings well in hand as we looked to Ann's return from college.

She arrived safely two days later despite unsafe weather through which to maneuver a small Volkswagen two hundred miles. We thanked God for her horn signal as she slowly climbed our driveway. She parked behind the unfamiliar old Buick. Our need to borrow transportation became the subject of conversation during dinner.

"Dad, you and mother take my car. I don't need it at school."

"Then we could return the Sheffield's car," Arline said.

"That's true, honey," I replied. "Even though they have given us no indication of wanting it back, I would prefer using our own car. And the only one left in this family is yours, Ann."

"I know that, Dad, and while I'm home all I need is a ride to and from work." Ann turned to Ken as he started to leave.

"Don't look at me, Ann. All I have is a bike."

"I didn't mean you, Kenny. I wouldn't be seen dead on that stupid bike of yours."

"Besides," Ken quipped as though Ann had not spoken, "I have no chains for it, and they don't make snow tires for ten-speeds."

"Very funny," she said without laughing. "At least I'm working on my vacation." Ken ignored her.

"Ann, your mother and I want you to know we really appreciate you working to help out during this hard time in our life."

"That's okay, Pop. And if I can't go back to school in January, I'll see about working full time."

"Let's not jump so far ahead." Arline demanded. "We don't have to pay the Boston bank the tuition loan right away, so you're not going to get thrown out of school that fast. And, your dad will probably have work by then."

I yearn for the fulfillment of Arline's prediction. Life

without income is debilitating. I daily question my talents. Can I really sell? Am I as good as I want to believe? Hundreds of tributes have been bestowed upon me throughout my exciting, although unsettled, life. From early combat flying successes to the top of selling achievements, I have been congratulated. Except for a few scathing remarks no longer remembered. And for one which I cannot forget.

During my first year of selling in Manhattan, I indirectly learned that a superior told one of my clients that he did not believe I was a good salesman. Hundreds of triumphant selling coups have not been able to erase that one negative comment. I carry it with me into every agency I solicit. One opposing expression has had more damaging impact upon my self-confidence than a thousand signed contracts. And it won't go away!

Settled into my subconscious, this seed of doubt finds nourishment through recognition and recall. In full bloom now, during this present period of my faltering career, doubt is having a vintage year. Is his malignant opinion regarding my talents true? Or is it that I do not sell as daringly without alcohol? Perhaps. In honest retrospect, I have never been fired during all those years of problem drinking. Only now. While sober. Previously I manufactured reasons for quitting. Now I look to contrive reasons for being hired. By anyone. But how can I use being fired as a welcomed, progressive step in my film career? I simply proclaim unemployment a step in the right direction. I don't have to believe it. Those to whom I speak have to believe it. Most don't.

"It seems we oversold in New York," I said proudly. "I saw the handwriting on the wall when California could not handle the cash flow. It was a matter of being under-capitalized and overbooked." The other end of the telephone did not respond. I continued to sell the most difficult product of all. Me.

"So if you need a hot salesman, I'm considering offers."

I played the game of Madison Avenue jobhunting. The

impression to leave is, "you can get me if you hurry." This chance to completely trust Christ was slipping away. I used the same weapons used by all out of work sales reps. I should be using my own weapons—of trust, honesty, and patience. Those given me by God. In employing their attitudes, they have won me to their methods. And I'm not going to win for any amount of money.

The telephone finally spoke. "Too much production and not enough cash can do it, Fred." He waited for me to agree. I could not. "And as much as we would like to hire a man of your reputation, I'm afraid we can't look at that possibility right now. It's slow this time of year, you know that. So why don't you call me in January. Or February. Conditions may have changed by then." Coolness in his voice told me he wanted to end the conversation. I ended the attempt with a promise to call again. I knew I would not. But I might just drop in one day.

Three days each week I commuted into Manhattan. I took later buses in and earlier buses out, but I remained somewhat visible in the mainstream of Madison Avenue film and advertising. The old gang at P.J.'s beckoned. I knew they would be sympathetic. Many have lived through more than one job cancellation brought about because a major client decided to leave their agency. Most of these men know how to survive when "on the beach" and out of work. If they lost their spirit at home because of temporary unemployment, they covered the loss well with different spirits when in P.J.'s. Although I didn't want to drink with them, I did want the carefree, holiday mood of their drinking. They welcomed me into the fold again. Into the womb of fellow sufferers. As one no longer infallible. They were surprised when I continued to order club soda. I wasn't. I didn't want to drink because I knew I didn't have to drink. I did have to appear unruffled by events. And somewhat solvent.

"I don't know about the rest of you guys, but I can only go three, maybe four, months without work," I exaggerated. "By then our savings will have had it."

"Have you got your resume with a good headhunter?" someone asked between drinks.

"I don't know a headhunter. Good or bad. I've never had to prepare a resume, either. But if that's a way to go, I'll do it. What do these guys do for you that we can't do ourselves?"

"Hopefully, they get you off unemployment," laughed a martini owner. "They're executive placement agencies. They know where the jobs are, so they try to put the proper head with the open position. They get you working."

"Quickly," said a voice in the pack.

I joined their laughter, but not their jokes. I became keenly aware that I'm no longer the free-spending, fast-selling, fun-drinking salesman of one year ago. I've lost my impact on these former clients. Two company failures in which I've been a part have cast a stigma of poor credibility. I may even find difficulty getting another job in advertising. Particularly one which will provide an income to match our wants. The thought of being moved out of New York City and film production shot through my mind. Yet I feel calm. I want to trust more in God's plans for us than in my concern to quickly solve our problem. I know, without hesitation, that drinking is not the solution. A stronger resolve to not drink emerges. It deepens my trust in Christ who has again protected my fragile gift of sobriety. I don't need this bar. I cannot find God's direction for me here. Much the same as a coal miner who cannot see beyond the lighted path of his helmet lamp until he takes another step, I cannot see God's light for great distances unless I'm willing to take each succeeding step. He'll light my way as long as I'm under way.

I recently learned God guides through areas and conditions we cannot manage alone. When we have been taken through the obstacle, he backs off and allows us to continue under our own power and command. Acts 12:10, 11 records Peter being led by an angel through barriers and dangers which he could not maneuver. When safely guided out of prison, the angel left. Peter was on his own. Then Peter's intelligence and knowledge of the Lord's leading took over. He continued alone to Mary's house. God had helped him to the point where he could carry on. Since he did it for Peter, I know God is anxious to help me through formidable barriers also. I believe he is keeping his promise today, just as surely. Fear of Christmas without money or job evaporates as I leave P.J.'s. This season is more exciting and joyful than any Christmas period I've experienced. And Christ had laid the groundwork six months ago.

Last July, with one full year of Christ under my heart, I dared go to a healing service in Elizabeth, New Jersey. Arline had read of the happening, and I wanted the adventure God presented. That midsummer Saturday, perfectly weathered for golf, became a day I would never forget. I cancelled play with my usual foursome and met one of the most altruistic twosomes I had ever encountered—and in one man.

Father Roy Hendricks, Rector of St. Stephen's Episcopal Church of Philadelphia never walked alone. Christ was always with him. I saw our Lord on Father Roy's face the moment he entered the huge sanctuary. And I felt Christ in me as I knelt, with Arline, before this man who was to become God's messenger to me. We asked for healing in a man whom we had not met, but for whom many of the "Monday lunch bunch" were praying. Roy Hendricks prayed as we requested. Then he prayed for a healing to take place in our lives. For a stronger bond between us. In our marriage. His perception overwhelmed us. We drove home in silence and spent the warm summer evening in awed discussion regarding our day in Elizabeth. During that tranquil time between sunset and total darkness, when noise of the day seems muffled in subdued light, God chose to prepare us for December.

Father Roy telephoned from his study in Philadelphia He called to tell us he could not forget us this day. He would be available to us whenever we called. We were invited to visit his great church soon. He passed on his belief that we would be used fully by God, . . . that we are his children and in his care. Filled with astonishing peace, we promised to keep alive this friendship so clearly given by God. Arline kept that promise through her great gift of letter writing, and I'm now, in December, able to call Father Roy for sympathy due me for being so unfairly cast upon the shores of those unemployed. He would surely understand.

Laughter greeted me from Philadelphia. I told Roy of our desperate circumstance. He laughed again. More heartily. I thought I had made connection with the wrong Father Roy.

"I'm delighted with the news, Fred. The Holy Spirit is really working in your life. You're a very fortunate man indeed."

"Fortunate? I know you're right, Roy. And I know the Lord is bringing good out of these days, and that I'm not drinking in spite of everything. But I feel so beat up."

"The Holy Spirit does not fight with gloves on," he laughed. "You're going to be all right. Just be patient. You haven't gone hungry yet, and you are not going to lose your house immediately. If at all. You're being put to the test. And you're going to pass. Now, get a pencil and paper. I'm going to give you the name and phone number of a special friend of mine. He lives close to you. I want you to call him tonight. Tell him we have spoken and tell him what you've just told me." And so it was that another messenger entered my life. I called Roland Spiotta.

I obediently repeated my narrative to Roland. Somehow it didn't sound as desperate after Roy. God's leading is more important. Roland guided me to Paul's letter to the Romans. This man on the telephone, whom I have not met, directs me to get my Bible. The miracle is that I get my Bible. Anxiously. Excitedly. What is the good news from God?

"Chapter eight, Fred. Read with me, beginning with the

twenty-fourth verse. 'We are saved by trusting. And trusting means looking forward to getting something we don't
yet have—for a man who already has something doesn't
need to hope and trust that he will get it. But if we must
keep trusting God for something that hasn't happened yet,
it teaches us to wait patiently and confidently.' "

How did Father Roy's friend know my need so quickly?
So precisely? Paul said to trust, and that's my weakness. I
don't trust Christ enough. And when I do, it doesn't last too
long.

"Thank you, Roland. You've zeroed in on the exact point
in which I find myself failing. I've read Romans, but I never
saw those words like this before."

"The Lord uses each of us to speak for him, Fred. Tonight he used me for your need. Perhaps you would like to
continue what we've started here tonight. A few of us have
a small prayer meeting once a week. You're welcome to join
us."

"I think I would like that. Can I bring my wife?"

Arline came with me, and the family circle God planned
for us grew. Each week we meet in fellowship and prayer
with Roland and new brothers and sisters. We became personally acquainted with Ralston Young and his wife, Sadie.
Ralston is Red Cap 42, Bishop of Grand Central Terminal,
friend of the late Sam Shoemaker, father of Faith at Work
and devoted friend of Bill W., co-founder of Alcoholics
Anonymous. Then our local Christian group, which grew so
beautifully from repeated weekend retreats, began weekly
small group meetings.

Within these suburban borough meetings we shared
God's demonstrative power in our otherwise destructive
financial crisis. As vividly as was seen by Israel in their
wilderness, we and those with whom we shared, saw the
hand of God in our desert. His manna for today is real.
Enough. Sustaining. Yet he gave us more. From within the
heart and mind of a neighbor, God provided greater measure.

"I just want you to know, Fred, that I'm good for a few

thousand if you need it," he said as we walked to his car. The gathering in our home this evening had left little doubt in any of us that Christ is alive in each person who opens their life to him and lets Jesus take over. "I've been waiting for the chance to tell you it's yours," he continued. "And don't worry about when or how you pay me back."

"I just can't take money from you like this," I stammered. "But I may have to. Why the magnificent offer?"

"Since I've taken the Lord into my life, I've put aside a fund to be used as he directs. Right now I feel you're the one it should be offered to."

"And that's all?"

"That's all. Except to keep it business like, I would appreciate it if you would sign a non-interest bearing note. To be paid back when you're able. We'll leave the payment date blank."

"Okay," I murmured. "I hope I can pay you back soon. But for now, you're an answer to prayer and a lot easier to deal with than State unemployment," I joked with embarrassment.

This generous Christian friend enabled us to pay an overdraft at the bank and to keep our lights burning and telephone alive. Ann proudly purchased the Christmas turkey, and the State of New Jersey provided money for additional food. Our manna came in bunches.

Arline's cousin, a young airline pilot, moved to our town when his company transferred him east. He and his wife, Jerrie, spent considerable time with us, and as Arline's only relatives nearby, they knew intimately our status and struggle. They too were used by God.

"We're leaving in the morning for Christmas in St. Louis, 'Cous,' " he said. "But before we go, we're leaving you this blank check. If you need it to make a mortgage payment, or for anything else, just make it out to the amount you need, and let us know when we get back."

"We can't take money from you, CK," Arline said.

"We'd take it from you if we needed it. You guys didn't

hesitate to take us in when we didn't have a place to stay until we found our home. Besides," he smiled. "We're family. And there aren't too many of us from Missouri in these parts. We've got to stick together."

December mortgage was late, but paid.

Christmas gifts are accumulating rapidly, and they're coming wrapped in packages of all sizes and shapes. From sources known only to God, but by messengers known to us. The Reverend Doctor William Howell Emery arrived unannounced. To deliver another miracle.

"What's our favorite pastor doing out so close to Christmas? Want some coffee?" I asked. "It'll only take a minute."

"Can't stop for coffee, Fred. I've come to drop off a Christmas card laid on my desk today. It's addressed to you two."

The "Christmas card" Bill handed me was in the form of a normal business size envelope. Typed across the front was reference to Second Timothy 3:14. Inside were twenty twenty-dollar bills. Four hundred dollars in cash splashed across our kitchen table.

"I can't tell you who gave this to me, but I can say they are not members of our church. They're friends who heard you may need some help. You don't even have to pay them back. But if you do, the money will again be passed on to someone else in need." He wished us a merry Christmas before rushing off. We went to Second Timothy 3:14. "But you must keep on believing the things you have been taught. You know they are true for you know that you can trust those of us who have taught you."

Trust again. There it is in confirmation. God's love and concern filled my eyes with tears and my heart with unbelievable gratitude. Every encounter with Christmas this first year of sobriety is assuring me I need not worry about tomorrow's bread. Or mortgage payments. And gifts, when his are so priceless. For how can one measure salvation? Or wrap it? What color the ribbon? One gift of salvation God gave to us was almost six feet high.

Kenneth Frederick Foster; age sixteen, five feet eleven inches tall, and still growing. A serious young man who loves his home, his school, and this quiet New Jersey suburb. Here he has grown to early manhood. Impressionable and curious, this avid young reader questions life. And never more seriously than tonight, this fourth consecutive evening in which we have watched one of Billy Graham's televised crusades.

Dr. Graham's theme has concentrated on Satan's power, and cunning influence on our distance from God. We have been keenly interested in the crusade's effectiveness in giving courage to thousands who dare come forward and publicly claim Christ as Savior. Unknown to Arline and me, Ken was no less moved. He wanted to come forward. To dare to believe. God used Billy Graham to spark Ken's need. He then used Arline to ignite a fire in Ken which only Christ could calm. And he used an act of brave obedience by Arline to wrap it all together in language he understands. She told us of a recent experience in direction from the Holy Spirit.

The surface of Arline's consciousness was flooded with God's revelation to her of the many items and games devoted to witchcraft and magic stored in this Christian home. Dutifully she found, and threw out, tarot cards, Ouija boards, and books relating to astrology. Six books on witches and their history, which had been sent unsolicited to Ann, thus found their way to our local dump. Moved to search our attic, Arline found a motherlode of forgotten books and old masks no longer needed in this joyous home of deepening faith in the spirit of Christ. She told us of her writing all this to Ann, for she felt she had thrown away Ann's property without the right to do so. Ann's response to her mother's letter revealed she and a few of her closer college friends questioned their own degree of faith when compared to the courageous example set by Arline in her victorious encounter with Satan. We were proud of Ann. That she too had courage enough to share her mother's unusual conviction, persuaded Ken to contribute to the household purifying. He dashed to his room. Upon returning he held a book.

"I've got to get rid of this," he exclaimed. "It's on exorcism and weird ways to make contact with spirits." He began tearing pages and fed them to the burning log fire. "After hearing Billy Graham tonight, and then your experiences, Mom, I want to know more about Christ."

We sat and watched the glowing fire consume Ken's now unwanted book. We spoke calmly of Christ and how we feel about our relationship with him. I could not help recalling last December. Extreme heavy drinking filled every waking moment then. Those last days of hell on earth for me and my family were reaching their final crescendo. My silent partner of so many drunks had tried his best to convince me then that I did not have a drinking problem. Christ defeated him then and is winning the conflict within Ken tonight.

"I know we haven't got too much money left, Dad. And I know you may not get another job right away. But," he added, turning to his mother, "you don't seem very upset about this."

"You're right, Ken. I'm not deeply upset. Most of the time, that is." Arline rested her hand on his arm. "I almost don't know why, other than I'm trying to live each day as it comes, and to trust Christ. I'm holding God to his promise that he will never forsake me. That he will never let go. And, as a born-again Christian, Ken, I know something good will come of this. I won't tell you, or your father, that I'm not frightened. I am. But I'm not afraid to face where Christ is using me. Do you understand what I'm saying, Kenneth?"

"I understand, and I want that kind of relationship with him because you two have changed. Besides you being sober much longer than I thought you were going to make it, Dad, there's something in both of you that you didn't have before."

"Christ really does live, Ken. Anytime you want to ask him to come into your life, to take charge, your mother and I, or either one of us, will help you find him."

"I think I want that right now," he whispered.

Ken's gift of salvation had been wrapped perfectly for him to receive it. We were used to lead our only son to God's only Son. The Christ of Christmas enveloped Kenneth Frederick Foster. Three hearts now thanked God for all our blessings, and prayed that Ann would soon open herself to know our joy. Our wealth.

God's unemployment compensation is overpowering. His gifts have given me courage and a deeper trust. A new determination to get back up, to charge into the New Year with confidence, surges through my body. My resume of job qualifications was lived and recorded for me two thousand years ago by a carpenter who was never without work. I don't need a resume for Christ. He's not my hired headhunter, commissioned to find the perfect job, with the perfect boss and the perfect salary. He's my Lord and Savior. He has a plan for my life. A plan for which I could never qualify on my own.

He called me while in Manhattan's untamed advertising kingdom. His gift, my acceptance of that call, made me a full-time heir to all of his kingdom's riches. Everything which is of God the Father is mine to claim as a son.

I do not believe his strategem for me includes many more visits before window "A to K."

*To dream
of the person
you would like to be
is to waste
the person
you are.*

INSCRIBED ON A
DEPARTMENT STORE
CLOCK.

START A NEW PAST

"The last thing in this world I want," Arline said, "is to leave this home. If the Lord is leading us to other places, I'm not happy with the thought."

"We're not going to lose this house, Arline," I tried to promise. "As soon as this week is over and the holidays are behind us, I'll be working. We've just been hit at the slowest time of the year in the film business, honey." If she heard she didn't believe.

"I don't know how we're ever going to be able to pay all the bills which have piled up. And in one more year, both Ann and Ken will be in college at the same time. Where's the money coming from for that? We can't even pay for Ann's." She paused and lowered her head. "Do you suppose the Lord is telling us to sell everything except that huge pot, and go into a retreat somewhere?" She didn't wait for my reply. "Fred, I don't want to be a missionary. I don't want to leave my home and all we've accumulated. This is the only thing we've had which has felt solid to me and the children. They've grown up here. And I've had my own dreams of them coming back to this house. With their families."

The precious enchantment of our best Christmas has passed. Reality is upon us this week between December 25 and January 1. The nearness of the year's first month—the back to work month—must be faced. Arline's fears permeate. They're my feelings. Unspoken. Of impending financial danger under the watchful care of God. We won't go hungry or without clothing and shelter, but we do fear our ability to cope with change for which neither of us feel prepared. Or want. Trust in Christ is not the issue. Our willingness to follow is the issue. To dare again. To become the person Christ sees. Not to remain the person I see of myself. I'm sober, and I believe God has that plan for my life. But I'm not certain I have courage enough to stay out of his way.

E. Stanley Jones explained the benefits of exercising complete faith when he wrote, "The man who believes absolutely in God, in the divine reliability and goodness, does not hold himself mentally and spiritually rigid, fearful that any moment something is going to happen to him, but, on the contrary, rests in complete confidence that all things work together for good to them who believe in God. As a result, he has peace in his mind and quietness at the center of his life. . . . This relaxed and peaceful state of mind gives him a clear brain, makes possible the free exercise of all his faculties, and thus he is able to attack his problems with every ounce of ability he possesses. The relaxed man is the powerful man."[14]

I want to be that man! I want to be able to face the coming year without the familiar feelings of inadequacy, guilt, and desperation. Convinced these days of fear are wrong, regardless of our predicament, I searched further into books I've read this past year. I scrutinized writing I had carefully underlined to better remember their messages. I needed to remember.

Last May, Robert Schuller's *Move Ahead with Possibility Thinking*, gave me an authentic belief in my ability to accomplish whatever reasonable goal I established, so long as I could take it to Christ for his guidance and endorsement. Not unlike E. Stanley Jones' relaxed and thus powerful man, Dr. Schuller prescribed a daily exercise of reading aloud certain positive statements to overcome negative thinking:

"I can do great things.

"I have great possibilities deep inside of me.

"I have possibilities that haven't been born yet.

"I'm really a wonderful person when Christ lives in me.

"I've been too self-critical.

"I've been my own worst enemy.

"I'm a child of God. God loves me.

"I can do all things through Christ who strengthens me."[15]

This reemphasis on God's power in my life today, and of my own choice of attitude with which I face each day, dragged me out of myself. Fred Foster, the bouncing ball of emotion, has returned to the positive side of life. The pity-party I had wallowed in and had enjoyed is over. Time has come for me to stop feeling sorry. For blaming circumstances. To know that Jesus Christ has not let go. That he's teaching me to be passive about the future, yet alert to each day's opportunities and challenges. Satan has a fight on his hands now. I know where to turn for the right kind of power. The switch of life is turned on. I'm learning, albeit slowly, to act without regard for feelings. To move in the direction of Christ *first*. I can save myself many heartaches if I would not wait until reaching the valley floor before looking up. For then I would see some of the rewards which have come during this first year of sobriety. From the vantage point of the mountaintop. And I would plainly see his hand.

I would recognize I'm content to face the rest of my life without alcohol. That's a plus. And I do understand myself

and my disease more than ever. Honesty, too, is becoming
somewhat comfortable. Lies are not needed to cover lost
hours and the guilt which comes from having lost them.
Everything does not revolve around me. I'm not the center. God is. Each day I'm better at living one day at a time.
And within each of these days, my relationship with Arline
and our children improves. Part of any good relationship is
being reliable, and I'm certainly more reliable than last
year at this time. I'm also able to help others, particularly
the drinking alcoholic who wants sobriety. And I'm doing
tasks for which I had little patience one year ago. I write
letters. Return phone calls. Keep promises. Rake leaves.
Burn hot dogs over a charcoal fire. Hang wallpaper. Listen.
And I don't have to be as perfect to begin a task.

The process is slow, but change is obvious when I look for
it. Old habits, which God wants removed, continually
annoy until positive action is taken. Cigarette smoking, now
up to two packs each day, plagues me. Once before I had
stopped. For over six years I abstained from tobacco of all
kinds. I want to stop again because I learned how God
wants me to treat my body.

"Haven't you yet learned that your body is the home of
the Holy Spirit God gave you, and that he lives within you?
Your own body does not belong to you. For God has bought
you with a great price. So use every part of your body to
give glory back to God, because he owns it." (1 Cor. 6:19,
20.)

The other day I knew I had to clean up his room.

Four of us sat around the kitchen table. Breakfast had
been leisurely and plentiful. We lingered over coffee and
cigarettes. Many cigarettes. Smoke filled the small kitchen.
Four lighted sticks of tobacco burning simultaneously
creates blue-colored air. I knew my family had been influenced by my smoking. So long as I smoke, they will follow
my lead. They may not stop if I stop, but I certainly set a
strong example. I focused on Ken.

"New Year's Eve is getting close, son. I haven't tried to

stop anything this year except drinking. That has been enough. And I was advised not to try to stop but one habit at a time. Now that my first year is about over, though, I would like to begin the New Year without smoking. I'm going to quit cigarettes." Arline, Ann, and Ken looked first at me, then to each other. Do they think I've gone crazy? Or that I'm still compulsive. I pressed on. "Ken, are you willing to try stopping with me? At the stroke of twelve tomorrow night?"

"Sure," he answered. "I'm just smoking because there isn't anything else to do. I can stop any time I want. In fact, Dad, I don't smoke during the day at all. Only when we're together. But if you want to stop together, that's fine. I'll stop with you."

"Okay, you've got a deal," I bargained. I had myself a partner. We shook hands and we both lit another fresh cigarette.

New Year's Eve marks the completion of one full year of not drinking. It ushers in the three hundred and sixty-sixth day of continual sobriety. And it presents a few new challenges. I pondered where we would be next Christmas. I knew I would watch the televised plunge of the electric ball on Times Square Tower again this year. The precise second through which the old passes, and the new begins, still grips my attention. It's the most striking demonstration of past, present, and future rolled into three seconds of time. This moment in time is cause for more drunken people to drink who believe they must become inebriated to fully enjoy the occasion. For those of us who have abused countless nights without cause, this night promotes resolve not to drink. Even during a large, rousing New Year's Eve party.

Noisemakers, paper hats, confetti, and inflated balloons filled every downstairs room of the spacious old home. The attorney and his wife who are hosting the joyous party have been friends for almost one year. His many years of continual sobriety, after near disaster from alcoholism, helped me many times in my fight. Forty or more other partygoers present tonight have similar experiences. Each has tasted new life. And this night of nights, when drunks are acceptable in their behavior, an inebriate cannot be found in this throng of happy people.

Wine and liquor can be seen. But not its abuse. Spouses of recovering alcoholics, and friends who drink normally, need not be denied simply because we cannot imbibe. Today's society abounds in alcohol. Those of us who are not able to stop after taking the first drink must learn to live in an atmosphere of readily available booze. It's a highly accepted drug. In the best of circles. More so than cigarettes in some. I was about to be accepted in both.

Cigarettes do not render the user unconscious, so my chainsmoking tactics of this last night of inhaling did not affect my ability to focus on television as past, present, and future rolled by with the sinking of an electric ball. Hundreds of thousands screamed in Times Square as I blew the last deep breath of smoke directly towards the television screen. I watched the smoke dissipate. Arline stood close. We kissed and wished each other a great new year.

"Happy first anniversary, honey," she smiled. "I'm so proud of you for this past year."

"It's a miracle, darling. Nothing short of a miracle. For me to put together three hundred and sixty-five consecutive days of not drinking has been possible only through God's strength."

"Are you really going to stop smoking now?"

"I'm going to try it one day at a time, honey. No promises. And I've turned the problem over to the Lord. He knows I want to stop the nicotine habit. Beside, Kenny and I have a pact. We're going to do it together. You've already stopped, and I love you very much for the encouragement, sweetheart."

"I wonder what the year holds for us, Fred. We could not be facing it more dependent on God than we are tonight."

"Are you frightened?"

"I'm not sure how I feel. When I think about what could happen if you ever got sick—real sick—I worry very much. Just what would we do, Fred?"

I spotted an empty couch, and guided Arline to it. "I don't know, honey. I'm not going to get sick, though. I'm as healthy as a horse." Her question stabbed with portentous truth. A truth from which I could not escape through club soda and ginger ale. I automatically reached for a cigarette. I threw the near full pack away. Another manmade crutch weakened its hold, and the beginning place from which my strength will come, and through whom the balance of my life must rest, converged. I'm becoming increasingly dependent upon God for all things, and now that the holidays are over, I must come out from under the cover of sympathy which abounds during this time of the year.

January. Cold, stark, back-to-normal January, is here. The Christmas tree is down. That corner of the living room, from which it radiated scent and light, returns to order. With the tree's demise, job hunting reappears. Familiar faces are seen on the morning bus. My search for God's plan intensifies. Rejection comes from all quarters except his.

"Sid, I know you've got a new company going now, so I thought I'd call to see if you could use me." Sidney Steen, former boss, and partner in the most financially successful television commercial film studio Manhattan had ever experienced, was abrupt and singularly business as we spoke over the phone. He offered a bone.

"Since the old company broke up, Fred, it's just been me and one of the directors. We don't need help in this town, but we're about to open a small video tape facility out on Long Island. It's to do some of the test commercial business around. Nothing big. But we may be able to use someone to sell that operation. It won't pay much, and it's probably not right for where you've come from."

"I don't think I could stand the commute, Sid. Long Island is too far from New Jersey, especially when I'd have

202 The Up & Outer

to travel all the way across town before even getting to the
Island. That's a two-hour trip each way." I found a logical
excuse for not jumping at the bone. We said good-bye, with
invitations to keep in touch.

This had been a most difficult call to initiate, but it had to
be made. All other studios were not interested. Eight in a
row did not need my efforts. Drunk or sober. Going back to
Sid Steen for help crushed the confidence I had received
from Christ in the morning. His disinheritance shamed.
Doubt regarding my reputation in our industry flourished.
Questions concerning Sid's knowledge of my past drinking
habits added to my headlong rush into dreaming about the
safe and secure confines of a retreat center, Christian
broadcasting of some form, or a monastery. God may be
leading me into a completely new life by closing doors to
the old. Where will the new doors open? It can't be a
monastery. I'm married. And Protestant.

During the next three weeks we kept an open mind to
God's leading. I called every Christian I could think of who
might be of help. Proverbs 15:22 told me, "Plans go wrong
with too few counselors; many counselors bring success." I
found the counselors needed. And vital prayer support.
Their concern for our welfare, and confirmation of our belief in God's promises strengthened us against total despair.
A significant contact for an interview regarding Christian
broadcasting sent us scurrying to Pennsylvania.

"Arline," I shouted. "I really think God is telling us to go
to Philadelphia. Perhaps we should talk to Billy Graham's
agency people, as that couple in Hartford advised. Listen
to this." I read Revelation 3:8. " 'I know you well; you
aren't strong, but you have tried to obey and have not
denied my Name. Therefore I have opened a door to you
that no one can shut.' " Exiled and alone on the island of
Patmos, John recorded Christ's directions regarding the
letter John was to write to the leader of the church in
ancient Philadelphia. Today's Philadelphia, the City of
Brotherly Love, is the home of Billy Graham's advertising

agency. Perhaps there I will find the door that no one can shut. I phoned and received an appointment for the next day. It was the third day of not smoking.

The door to Christian broadcasting did not shut in Philadelphia. It simply did not open. Yet we were not seriously disappointed. A pleasant, and lengthy, meeting with the Graham advertising staff had not produced an offer of work. Nor a feeling in either of us that we had missed an opportunity. The journey was not in vain, for I did experience two positive convictions: I could sit through hours of closed door conversation, in an advertising agency, without smoking. And I knew I wanted to follow the Lord as closely as I'm able to discern his will. I exercised obedience today, and thus stepped a little closer to his steering. All of this in one day certainly makes it a special day. It has not helped pay those bills. January mortgage, all utility bills, and college loan payments recycle every four weeks. And they do not come as a surprise to God. He keeps his promises.

The settlement for $1500 arrived from California, and Bill Emery stopped by for more coffee. Again he bore gifts.

"Fred, our board of deacons has a fund from which they grant loans to people temporarily in need. They have asked me to check with you to see if you could use some help. Are you interested? And how much do you need? And I'd love a cup of coffee."

"Sit down and take a breath, Bill. You're going so fast I'm not sure what I just heard."

"Can you use some money? That's what I asked."

"A thousand dollars would keep us going until the end of the month, Bill. Do you suppose they would go for that much?"

They did. Our hard working friend, and pastor, spoke to our Board of Deacons. They believed elders Fred and Arline good risks. Now we have two $1000 notes and four hundred dollars in a most timely Christmas card to return. But our home is secure for another thirty days, and there's a full tank of heating oil sunk beneath our back lawn. Ann is back in college, and the wolves knocking at our door have not as yet displayed teeth. Only threatening growls.

I'm driven to search more relentlessly for work in the only marketplace I know well, New York City film production. I may feel it has shut me out, but I do not believe God wants me to hang around in New Jersey doing nothing during this period of seeking to do his will my way. He may want me to remain in television. To be his witness there. It's the most difficult setting I know in which to present Christ. If film production is my area of ministry, then I'd best get on with finding the job he has in it for me. I completed my resume, the first, and took to the streets of midtown Manhattan. Soon February threatened. The wolves were restless. They were showing a few teeth.

Fierce January temperatures took their toll on our home heating oil. A refill would be needed in ten days. After two hours of aimlessly wandering around Madison and Park Avenues, I headed for P. J.'s. There I can get a good hamburger and talk to someone I know. I won't feel so lonely. And the telephone is close by. While waiting to cross Lexington Avenue, my attention was captured by someone calling my name above the street noise. I turned to meet a film director with whom I had worked ten years ago.

"I'm on my way over to P. J.'s, Fred," he called.

"So am I. I'll walk over with you." We shook hands.

"You won't believe this, but the reason I'm heading to that joint is to see if I could find you, and if not, to get your home phone number from one of the gang. I've heard about you being on the beach, and I want to talk to you."

I kept calm. He must not sense my need. "Would you rather we don't go to P. J.'s then? We can talk someplace else," I offered.

"No, that's okay. As a matter of fact, what I have to say won't take any time at all. I just want to see if you'd be at all interested in working with me. I really need a guy like you to sell me in this town. As you know, it has not been too easy for me. People still think of me as the wild, uncontrollable guy of five years ago. And it's not so."

"Have you changed that much?" I questioned between pounding heart beats I knew he could hear.

"I think so. I've resolved most of my inner conflicts about the business, and I'm not letting people get to me so readily. I do my own thing, Fred, and that's all I can give. If my client doesn't like what I contribute to a shoot, then I simply do it his way, and my way if time permits."

I could contain the all important question no longer. "What kind of a deal would you be talking about for me if I came with you?" I asked.

"Why not what you were making with the California outfit? I know you don't come cheap. Only let's handle it as a draw. That way I don't have to get involved in withholding taxes and all that sort of garbage. You be a self-employed sales service to me. It will also help my cash flow. You do your own taxes and take care of your own medical insurance. Okay?"

"That's fine with me," I said as unemotionally as I could. "When do I start?"

"You've just started." We shook hands again as we walked against the cold February wind. "Let's go have lunch with some of our clients," he said. I appreciated his emphasis on "our" clients.

This walk of only a few city blocks brought to a close my urgent search. The day is revitalized. I'm back on the labor force. I'm gainfully employed. I must call Arline. Window "A to K" is at an end for me. I've shortened the line there, and lengthened the line at our bank's deposit window. The house need not be sold. The huge retreat pot in our basement must wait another call. I've been called away. Called into what became the most trying selling berth of my career. I would need every day of the thirteen months of sobriety to sustain me. If I had come to this job while drinking, I might have died.

Although a benefactor, and an answer to prayer, this extremely talented film director became the fulcrum around which revolved the most bizarre selling conditions experienced in fifteen years of beating the pavements of Chicago and New York. It began within our first lunch as I stood in front of P. J.'s well-trodden bar, drinking a club soda spiked with fresh lime. Hours passed. We never did get to eat. Many drinks, and toasts in celebration of my new job and his expanding company, were offered. Glasses were raised and refilled by my employer. At three o'clock, now soggy from countless nonalcoholic drinks, I announced my departure. We chose ten-thirty tomorrow morning as the appointed time for me to arrive at his apartment. Strange, I thought. Why not the office?

Park Avenue and Seventy-first Street is a pleasantly superior neighborhood. Streets are clean. Broad. A center divider yields, in turn, spring flowers, fall colors, and a strip of genuine dirt upon which winter can dump snow which will not be ground to dirty water under the wheels of Manhattan's daily auto stampede. It's also the address of my director's plush bachelor apartment.

After considerable delay, the uniformed doorman announced my arrival. A sleepy, unshaved television commercial film director opened the seventeenth floor apartment door. His appearance surprised me. I believed we would leave immediately and go to the company's business office. I had been curious about the type and size of my new office. About my desk. A secretary. Even a couch with a coffee table. The visions I held during this morning's bus ride from New Jersey didn't come close to reality.

"Is it ten-thirty already, Fred? C'mon in."

"I'll wait downstairs if you'd like."

"Why would you wait downstairs? No, no. C'mon in. The place is a little messed up, but the cleaning gal will be here at eleven. Let me show you where you'll work, and where the coffee is kept."

He led the way, while I saw mortgage payments being made, full tanks of heating oil and all our other financial concerns met. Then I saw the kitchen, and smelled last night's cigarettes and liquor. They permeated the hallway and became stronger in the small cooking area. He walked into an adjacent room. I followed.

"We'll just use this bedroom for now, Fred. Later, if you like, we can put a desk in it and make it look more like an office." He turned back into the kitchen. "Sorry Tom didn't make his bed before leaving. You know Tom Morrison, don't you?" I nodded. "Well, he's staying with me for a few weeks. He and his wife have split." I found New York's good Samaritan.

This small bedroom, overlooking back alleys seldom viewed by those who walk stately Park Avenue, housed an unmade single bed which appeared to have lost a violent struggle. Set against a back wall, it hugged the floor, cowering from another onslaught of restless sleeping. It need not fear me. I'm simply looking for a corner from which to make phone calls. And for a desk more traditional than the end table upon which sat "my" telephone. Office tradition could not be found in this confused, plush apartment. Lavishly supplied with expensive liquor, wine, and cordials, this suite is not conducive to an attitude of earnest selling.

I cleared counter space in the kitchen and made coffee before the cleaning lady arrived. A 16-millimeter film projector caught my eye. I placed it on the end table and began projecting sample reels of his work against the bedroom wall. It made a fine screening room.

"Do you think you can sell me with those commercials?" he interrupted.

"Sure. As a matter of fact, you've got an excellent reel. We should do well with it." I shut off the projector. "Do you want to brief me in on each spot? I'd like some background on how you did them, who was involved, where it was shot, and something about the agency people on the job. I'll need some answers before taking it into the street."

"We'll go through all of them. But not now. Let's go to lunch while this place gets back in shape." A vacuum cleaner sounded from an unknown front room.

P. J.'s repeated yesterday. Only more boring. I had heard all the industry news and gossip then. The group at the bar had heard about my day-old job. I had no desire to drink alcohol in any form, so I stood and tried to listen. To find a point of interest. A challenge in my new director. Or even an opening in their conversations which would allow a mild reference to working with us soon. It's difficult to sell a director's talents when he's present. He does his own selling simply by occupying a bar stool and picking up drink checks. Thirteen months sober, and my only source of income enjoys having me with him in bars. He's in no hurry for my first sale. I'm in a hurry to leave. I put my hand upon his shoulder to draw attention.

"I'm anxious to see the rest of your reels, so I'm going to head back to the apartment. I'll spend as much time as the day allows looking through everything. Then I'll have some questions for you in the morning."

Without a word, he turned and handed me keys. An affirmative nod, a lone salute, and a thumbs-up signal sent me on my way. Falling snow and early darkness greeted me on Third Avenue. God had released me from the lion's den. I identified with Daniel.

Two hours of viewing commercials convinced me I had a most unusual talent to sell. His ability to direct people, to tastefully decorate sets, to cast acting talent, and to obtain striking camera angles is outstanding. That he also produced and organized all his own shoots, and was highly respected for his honesty, added to my sense of esteem for this man's creative genius. I regretted knowing how much he liked gin martinis. And the quantity he seemed to need. Both were evident when he came in.

Tom Morrison, house guest and former client, accompanied him. Introductions were not necessary. I've known Tom for over five years. We have never worked together. We've only drunk together. And he has not believed my continued sobriety is serious. He expected I would slip back into what appears to him as normal drinking. My failure to do so I credit to God's protection. Each morning, in doses never before received, I'm filled with resolve not to drink. To seek opportunities to witness. The latter is more difficult. Not drinking takes its toll though, for it affords me many hours of lonely phone calling. And my spine refuses to align itself with the object upon which I constantly sit.

Tom Morrison's bed and I become well acquainted. Hour upon hour I sit on his bunk making calls. Initially my legs began to feel the squatted position. Subsequently my back reacted to the unusual stance. The effect is as though I sat on a very low chair all day. To stretch my legs, and thus straighten my backbone, I either push them lengthwise in front of me, or stand. Relief also comes when I've succeeded in getting appointments to show our work to agency producers. Selling dates give me reason to get out of my bedroom/office. To move.

The third day of work, I arrived at 8:45. The apartment was dark and quiet when I entered. A check of the back bedroom revealed Tom Morrison still asleep in my "office." On my "desk" and "chair." Those in the master bedroom at the front of the apartment had not heard me come in. Obviously life here starts much later.

Soon after this early morning arrival, it was suggested I not come to work before ten. And I could leave by four each afternoon. These hours thankfully made the day quite short and gave the two bachelors time to get their teeth brushed, hangovers under control, and plans made for the next evening. They gave me cause for unrest.

Our bills were now being paid, and we were thinking of buying a car of our own. I could not complain about the amount of income we were enjoying, nor the abundance with which God gives. The human side of me, however, did not feel secure working under these loose arrangements. I cannot feel a strong sense of contributing when the person from whom I'm collecting salary doesn't show a daily need for the fruits of my efforts. I knew I would not be a part of this organization too long.

Deep concern and doubt regarding my stature in Madison Avenue advertising circles follows daily. I'm not fearful. I'm expectant. God does have his hand upon me. Of this I'm certain. I just don't know how long I'm to fight the battle in New York. A born-again Christian doesn't seem to fit. Satan is not winning the battle within me, but he sure has conquered most of the twenty-four-dollar island. I'd like to get away from this city's negative influence. From the guilt I feel for not witnessing more. To have a goal. Drinking always provided the state through which I conjured goals. But sobriety is facing reality. And when one has dreamed most of his life away in frivolous search for unrealistic goals, reality is frightening. But not devastating. Especially when I share today's fears with another Christian removed from my immediate family.

As the "Monday lunch bunch" meetings continued, varying degrees of faith and devotion to Christ emerged. Some men admitted they continued attending only because they were afraid not to come. Others showed up when they felt the need. And a few came because they wanted Christ to shine through them for others to see. Such is the ministry of one of the original members, who first spoke of his love for Christ during an early meeting in the old brownstone. Since that time, his fashionable Park Avenue beauty salon has become his mission field. Without annoying, or pushing, he's ready to witness at the drop of a curler. He talks of Jesus Christ to all who will listen. When this stylist friend of mine heard of my new commuting schedule, he suggested we travel together. One morning he asked if I would be interested in stopping for prayer. He knew of a beautiful church on the corner of Sixtieth and Park. I accepted. Immediately.

Our homes in New Jersey were only two blocks from each other. On those days when he did not drive into the city, he picked me up and we took a train. Either way, new hours were granted to us for sharing. I told him all of my concerns about New York and God's leading there. He, in turn, allowed me secrets of his heart. And we grew. We grew also to love the time God gave us together.

On those days of commuting by train, we surface on the streets of New York from the subway. A short walk takes us to the Park Avenue church. Inside one of the most beautiful sanctuaries I have ever seen, we kneel. Silently we pray. For each other. For our families. Customers and clients are claimed. My boss and his house guests do not escape our petitions. Empty of ourselves and filled with power, we step onto Park Avenue taller, by far, than when we entered. Another day can be faced from a full heart and absolute confidence in God's promises. Doubt about my career in film and advertising does not change. But fear regarding our future ebbs, as God fills me with joy. And that peace I could never before capture.

As I walked up Park Avenue en route to work, the first warm sunshine of spring is felt through my topcoat. Hope is in my heart. New York casts a brighter hue. Fifteen months of delicate sobriety through the miracle which is Christ will not be jeopardized this day. I've promised God I will not drink before going to bed. A lifetime of irresponsible running focuses now upon the steadfastness of God within this twenty-four-hour period, and I think again of Christian broadcasting. Of my desire to be in it. And out of this type of selling. Pat Robertson and his Christian Broadcasting Network in Portsmouth, Virginia, comes to mind.

I questioned why they have not responded to a letter I wrote last December. In it I presented an idea for a television show. The format of a Christian cooking show was not that bad. It was worth a reply. At least. But would Arline have moved to Portsmouth if they had bought my concept?

I know God is influencing her mind as he is mine. Perhaps a move from the anchor, which is New Jersey, is not an impossible thought.

I inserted the key and opened the door to my Park Avenue "office." Tonight I will call Pat Robertson.

It's time our past took on a new look.

*Christianity
is not a status
at which one arrives;
it is a life
in which one
matures.*
KEITH MILLER[16]

215

12

OF WINE AND FISH

"Arline and I are leaving for Portsmouth, Virginia," I declared. "So I won't be driving into New York with you this morning."

To help calm the shocked expression on the face of my hair stylist commute and prayer partner, I told him the sequence of this morning's experience. My conduct needed qualifying.

"Fred," he said shaking his head. "You are the most trusting Christian I know. Don't you realize this search could take you out of this part of the country?"

"Yes, but I have no choice. At least not in this matter. I've already called my boss and told him I would be out for at least three days, so please try to understand." He smiled and slowly moved his head in the affirmative. "We simply feel," I continued, "the Lord is trying to tell us something significant."

"Are you just driving down, or are you going to see someone when you get there?"

"I just spoke with a John Gilman in Portsmouth. He's program director for Pat Robertson's Christian Broadcasting Network. He wants us to come down and talk to him about a possible position with them. And we're to be guests on their 700 Club show tonight."

Convinced we could not be stopped, he bid me goodbye, wished us a safe journey, and asked God to be with us each mile of the way. I stepped quickly into the house. Bags need to be packed.

John Gilman had tried to call us this morning as we were inquiring about Pat Robertson's phone number. When our call got through, we were told Pat Robertson wanted us to talk with Mr. Gilman. I did not fathom the extent of John's surprise when he learned I was on the phone, calling him. We could not pass as simple coincidence John's failure to get us, and our success in getting him, within minutes of each other's efforts. He appeared to have run into stumbling blocks thrown at him by my silent adversary, and former accomplice, of past drinking forays. Satan convinced John our telephone number had been given to another subscriber who, when he called, screamed high-pitched obsenities, and babbled incoherently during his two attempts to locate us. I repeated our phone number to John. He assured me it was the same number he had just tried.

My call to Virginia, prompted by Arline's disclosure of God's word to her this morning, convinced John and me that his failure to make contact, after three months of not being able to respond to my December letter, was a deliberate act of Satan. He thus invited us to be guests on the next day's 700 Club. Aroused by this morning's events, and certain they are word from God, we eagerly accepted his proposition. We would go south.

Television or film sound stages are identical in physical character. And there's a special smell to their atmosphere. Before entering most stages, one moves past production offices, coffee machines, and thick soundproof doors. Each time I set foot on any stage, the immensity of space first astounds me. Then their realistic sets, from a simple kitchen to a complex chemist's laboratory, stirs my imagination. I'm in whatever world a set wants me. Instantly. Possessively. CBN's stages are no exception. Their equipment and atmosphere are identical. But that's where the likeness ends. The people staffing this southern command center for God's Word separate it from every other stage I've seen. Unconfined verbal praises to the Lord sound loudly and unexpectedly. Cameramen, acting talent, and technicians proclaim his name when they express joy and accomplishment. Exclamations to his moment-by-moment influence in their work and lives ignites a new, overwhelming longing that I be done with commercial film production. I'm a freed Christian filmmaker. I should be free to make Christian films, where I too can proclaim my relationship with Christ fearlessly. Unapologetically. Pat Robertson and John Gilman must be made to realize this—to want my years of experience, my production intellect. And spiritual enthusiasm. They considered all of me. On video tape.

Arline and I sat with Pat before his television cameras as guests on the 700 Club. My alcoholism, and Arline's living with it, were the theme of Pat's interview. I thanked God Arline was here, for her unequivocal recognition of my disease being a family affliction, shed a light on the problem most families do not see. Her calm responses to Pat's probing made it possible for me to contribute without being the subject. Alcoholism the disease, in me now dormant, was the subject. I became the catalyst. Arline the ensnared. But both recovering.

We watched the show's broadcast that night in our hotel room, uncertain of tomorrow's meeting with Pat Robertson and John Gilman. And our future. As an anonymous wise man once put it, "I do not know what the future holds, but I know who holds the future," we too know. So we try to live one day at a time. On faith. And better tomorrows.

We had lunch with Pat. Just the three of us. I told him of my years in the film business and of my need to become fully involved in Christian broadcasting. He listened. And affirmed. Arline bravely offered she would move if required. My gifts were discussed and recognized. But only partially unwrapped through Pat's suggestion that the network will soon need, and may be able to support, a creative director. The position would be a new one. He and John had talked about it, but were not moved to seek the person for the job. The idea excited me greatly, but Pat could not commit himself to hiring me. He asked for time to pray about the union. I felt comfortable with this plan. Arline was not positive Portsmouth was for us, and I wanted her further input as well as Ann's and Ken's. Ken gave us his conclusions upon our arrival home.

"You two are really something," he said as he closed the door behind us. After placing our suitcases at the foot of the stairs, he said, "When I got home from school Monday, and read your note about going to Virginia to see Pat Robertson, I couldn't believe you packed and left so fast. I'm sure glad you called me when you got there. I didn't know what happened to you."

"We felt the Lord was telling us to go. Doors seemed to be opening fast, so we packed immediately and drove down," I tried to reason.

"I gathered that when I read the Bible verse you mentioned in your note, Mother. But I don't think, from that verse, you were being directed by God to just go south as you said."

"Oh?," Arline exclaimed. "We clearly felt his direction. God was telling Philip to go south, and since Virginia is certainly south, we went to Virginia." I agreed with Arline.

"But you didn't read the whole verse. God told Philip to go south all right, but it was south to the desert road. At least that's what I read from my version. And Virginia is not desert."

"Go get it, son. I'd like to read that," I said. And then, "Which one are you studying?"

From his *New American Standard Bible*, Ken read Acts 8:26, the verse to which Arline had been directed during her morning reading and prayer two days ago. She had then impatiently showed the verse to me because we had been discussing Pat Robertson's work in Portsmouth. "But an angel of the Lord spoke to Philip saying, 'Arise and go south to the road that descends from Jerusalem to Gaza.' (This is a desert road.)"

"That's what we did, Ken." I said. "We went south."

"I also thought you were right until last night. Then you got a call from a studio out in California. In Los Angeles." Arline's eyes met mine as Ken continued. "Then I checked the map. Los Angeles is much further south than Portsmouth, Virginia. And, if it wasn't for irrigation, most of Southern California would be nothing but desert! The Bible verse said desert road. I think we're being directed to look to Los Angeles."

"Los Angeles," Arline protested.

"Who was the call from?" I asked.

"It's in the kitchen. By the phone. A man who seemed to know you. He was very nice. Wanted to know all about me and school. I told him where you and mom went, but that I didn't know when you would be back. He told me to ask you to call him, collect, whenever you got back. He sounded real anxious to reach you. Even left his home phone number."

"Are you going to call him, Fred?" Arline asked.

I looked at the phone message before answering Arline. The company name is very familiar. Their New York office had talked to me about working for them two years before.

"I'll call them tomorrow. I'm curious to know why they're calling from California."

Portsmouth and California gave rise to deep thoughts about my life over the past two years. It's been a long way from that night of near attack on Forty-second Street. I wondered about those two assailants whose knife point in my side gave me cause to overcelebrate in the safety of the bus terminal bar. And memory of that three-day retreat, when overlooking the Hudson River, I let go of running my life and gave it to Christ, brought guilt I still feel for the following six months. Had it been possible for me to profess Jesus as Lord and continue to drink daily? To each day surrender to God, then continue the fight with booze? Alone. Fish and wine, so often recorded in Scripture as life sustaining necessities, were my Saturday poison. Strange, I recalled, that during these sixteen months of sobriety, in which almost seventy Saturday's have come and gone, I have not had fish for lunch one time. And it was when I discontinued the "drinking man's diet" that I lost weight. And gained Arline's love again.

Mornings now are no longer spent trying to piece together yesterday. The same bedroom in which I now open my eyes reveals a life coming together. Furniture does not seem to stare in disbelief. When I slide my foot over to Arline's side of our queen-sized bed, cold emptiness is not my reward. Warmth. Life. Love. These have come from sobriety and Christ. Arline is at my side. The guest bedroom has not seen her. Or me.

Devotional and prayer time each morning is now my source of nourishment. So long shunned and looked upon by me as disgusting weakness, dialogue with God and reading, reading, reading slowly replace old habits. And new ones are born.

Mark Twain said, "The man who does not read has no advantage over the man who cannot read." Although I read often in the past, I didn't have much of an advantage because of what I read. The junk I read could not contribute to new life. In times of strife, only the standard which is Christ survives to become challenge instead of defeat. Living with the living Lord is life continually expanding. Yesterday's accomplishments are not good enough for today. And the good of today will not be good enough for tomorrow.

My appetite to uncover God's surprises is fed daily. And denied only when I choose to shut the door to his storehouse. Then I go hungry while fighting the Source because I'm ashamed to ask for more. I have asked for and received enough, I think. In fact, more than I deserve. And the nature which tells me I'm undeserving sets up the pattern through which I confine the nature of God in me. Although I impose my limited reasoning on God, he is not rendered incapable. Just Fred. So nothing important happens to me when all I look at is what I want and what I think will be endorsed by God so that it becomes his will for me.

I look to Christian broadcasting as the perfect setting for speaking and living for Christ. I want that to be God's will so I'll feel comfortable leaving the marketplace in which I find it difficult to speak his name. Bruce Larson charged me to remain in advertising when he wrote, "We must dispense with the myth that commitment to Christ means becoming a clergyman or that work done inside a church building or in a church organization is more holy, somehow, than work done in the marketplace. Christ came to give us a sense of calling in everyday work. This is where the world is changed, and where the Kingdom is built."[17] It was time to call John Gilman and talk to him about Christian broadcasting and my role in it. While dialing the Portsmouth exchange, I nervously fingered the California call-back number.

"John, Arline and I have put this decision to prayer every day since we saw you and Pat. Now, I realize that you folks have not made an offer. But before you do, let me say we do not feel at peace about joining CBN. I think God wants me where I am."

"The Lord continues to amaze me, Fred," he said. "We have talked and prayed about you coming down, and we too feel it's not what he wants. At least at this time. I have been concerned about telling you. That you'd be disappointed."

"Well, you don't have to fret, John. Maybe someday we'll work together. And if not, it's great to have met two more men with whom I'm going to spend eternity. So, if I don't get to see you here, John, we'll still be spending much time together."

"What do you plan to do?" he asked.

"We're not sure, but when you and I finish talking, I'm

going to call California." I told him all I knew of the person and the company which had called. Then, with his blessings, I put in a collect call to Los Angeles. The company operator knew my name and accepted the charges without delay.

Roy Keyes, president of one of the largest and most active commercial film production companies in California, asked if I was interested in working with him as executive vice president and executive producer. My mind whirled.

"Would it mean a move to California?" I asked.

"Yes, the job is out here. We would, of course, pay for your move. But before that happens, we'd like to have the New York office issue a plane ticket for you to come out and talk to us about it. Can you?"

"Yes, I can arrange that. But before I make the trip, Roy, I've got to know if I'm being interviewed for the job, or is the job mine if I decide to take it?"

"The job is yours if you want it," came his reply.

"Then issue two tickets. I'd like Arline to come with me. This is a family affair." He agreed.

Six blue eyes looked up at me from the kitchen table. Their expressions conveyed a trust I had never before seen. Or deserved. I placed the phone in its cradle and sat. No one spoke. They know a life-altering decision can be made at this moment in time. The magnitude of the conversation with California staggered us into a silence from which I felt love. We were bonded as a family more solidly than ever. I know now that as long as we remain together as a family, struggling, we'll weather all storms, no matter where they come from.

But California? Three thousand miles from life as we have known it for fifteen years? From friends? church? school? And from this home in which Arline and I have seen Ann and Ken grow. The home from which we would never move? I dared to break the silence.

"Well, who wants to go south? Unto the desert road?"

FOOTNOTES

CHAPTER TWO
1. Robert H. Schuller, *Move Ahead with Possibility Thinking* (Garden City, NY: Doubleday & Company, Inc., 1967), p. 77.

CHAPTER THREE
2. Dietrich Bonhoeffer, *Life Together* (New York: Harper & Row, 1954), p. 96.
3. A.A. World Services, Inc., *Alcoholics Anonymous* (New York: Alcoholics Anonymous World Services, Inc., 1955), p. 24.

CHAPTER FOUR
4. Jack B. Weiner, *Drinking* (New York: W. W. Norton & Company, Inc., 1975), p. 6.

CHAPTER FIVE
5. E. Stanley Jones, *Abundant Living* (Nashville: Abingdon, Festival Edition, April 1976), p. 43.
6. Roy L. Smith, *You Are Important* (Nashville: The Upper Room, 1952), p. 95.

CHAPTER SIX
7. Lloyd John Ogilvie, *Let God Love You* (Waco, TX: Word Books, 1974), p. 137.

CHAPTER SEVEN
8. Jones, *Abundant Living*, p. 42.
9. Pastor Paul, *Alcoholism* (Elgin, IL: David C. Cook Publishing Company, 1973), p. 181.
10. Judson Cornwall, *Let Us Praise* (Plainfield, N.J.: Logos International, 1973), p. 75.

CHAPTER EIGHT
11. Smith, *You Are Important*, p. 49.

CHAPTER NINE
12. Oliver Wendell Holmes, cited in *Proverbs to Live By*, ed. by Gail Peterson (Kansas City: Hallmark, 1975).
13. Every Monday, for over five years, this group of Manhattan businessmen met in the same room. A few have stopped attending. New men have replaced those who are gone. The "Monday lunch bunch" continue to brown bag it and to praise the Lord.

CHAPTER ELEVEN
14. Jones, *Abundant Living*, p. 245.
15. Schuller, *Move Ahead with Possibility Thinking*, pp. 34, 35.
16. Keith Miller, *The Taste of New Wine* (Waco, TX: Word Books, 1965), p. 109.

CHAPTER TWELVE
17. Keith Miller and Bruce Larson, *The Edge of Adventure* (Waco, TX: Word Books, 1975), p. 128.